Wulf Werum
Hans Windauer

Introduction to
PEARL

Programm Angewandte Informatik

Herausgeber:
Paul Schmitz
Norbert Szyperski

Wulf Werum/Hans Windauer:
PEARL, Process and Experiment Automation
Realtime Language

Wulf Werum/Hans Windauer:
Introduction to PEARL
Process and Experiment Automation
Realtime Language

Joachim Kanngiesser:
Die Abrechnung von ADV-Systemleistungen

Eric D. Carlson/Wolfgang Metz/Günter Müller/
Ralph H. Sprague/Jimmy A. Sutton:
Display Generation and Management
Systems (DGMS) for Interactive
Business Applications

Wulf Werum
Hans Windauer

Introduction to PEARL

**Process and Experiment Automation
Realtime Language**

Description with Examples

Friedr. Vieweg & Sohn   Braunschweig/Wiesbaden

CIP-Kurztitelaufnahme der Deutschen Bibliothek

Werum, Wulf:
Introduction to PEARL: process and experiment
automation realtime language; description with
examples/Wulf Werum; Hans Windauer. —
Braunschweig; Wiesbaden: Vieweg, 1982.
   (Programm Angewandte Informatik)
   ISBN 978-3-528-03590-7   ISBN 978-3-322-85763-7 (eBook)
   DOI 10.1007/978-3-322-85763-7
NE: Windauer, Hans:

Cover design: Peter Morys, Wolfenbüttel

ISBN 978-3-528-03590-7

PREFACE

PEARL (Process and Experiment Automation Realtime Language)
is a general purpose high order language designed to meet the requirements
of realtime programming in all fields of process and experiment automation
by means of computers.

PEARL has been developed in the period from 1969 until 1976 by cooperation
of German manufacturers (e.g. AEG , BBC , Siemens), software and systems
houses (e.g. ESG , GEI , GPP , IDAS , mbp , Werum), scientific institutes (e.g.
Hahn-Meitner-Institute of Berlin, Nuclear Research Centre of Jülich,
Universities of Erlangen, Heidelberg and Stuttgart) and users, organized
by GMR - VDI/VDE, the German association of engineers. The development
has been managed by the project PDV of the Kernforschungszentrum
Karlsruhe GmbH; it has been supported by the Federal Ministry of Research and Technology of Germany. More detailed information about
history and applications of PEARL can be read in Martin 78 and Martin 81.

In mid 1978 the draft standard of Basic PEARL was published (Standard 78).
This standard defines that subset of the full language PEARL, which has to
be common to all PEARL implementations. The draft standard of Full PEARL
was finished in mid 1980 (Standard 80).

Since 1979 the PEARL Association cares about PEARL activities of
common interest, especially about interests of PEARL users.

This language reference manual describes a subset of Full PEARL, which
contains in addition to Basic PEARL those language features of Full PEARL
necessary for elegant and efficient programming of complex applications.
In principal only those features of Full PEARL are not considered, which
require additional storage and administration effort at runtime. The extensions and restrictions in contrast to Basic PEARL and Full PEARL, resp.,
are listed in the appendix.

For this language Werum developed a portable compiler, which has been used by Werum and other institutions to implement the language on the computers

-   Amdahl 470/6 (for cross compilation)
-   Hewlett Packard HP 1000
-   Hewlett Packard HP 3000
-   INTEL 8086
-   Norsk Data NORD 10 , NORD 100
-   RDC   (a Really Distributed Computer Control System;
            see Syrbe 78 and Steusloff 80)
-   Siemens 404/3
-   Siemens 310
-   Siemens 330, R 30
-   Siemens 7.760 (for cross compilation).

The manual consists mainly of three parts: first, the introduction characterizes the "new" features of PEARL, i.e. the most important differences to older high order languages like FORTRAN or PL/I. For reasons of good understanding the second part describes only those features necessary to write simple programs. Additional possibilities are presented in the third part, which is followed by selected references to literature. For further references see Martin 78, Martin 81 and Kappatsch 79.

The appendix contains a list of all keywords, a table showing the valid possibilities to use the data types and a complete syntax description. (In order not to confuse the reader, the paragraphs often don't define the complete syntax of a language feature.) Paragraph 4 and 5 of the appendix list the extensions and restrictions in contrast to Basic PEARL and Full PEARL , respectively. The manual is closed by an index.

The language reference manual presented here is a translation of Werum 78 taking into account most recent standardization results (Standard 80).

CONTENTS

Part I

Introduction

1. IMPORTANT LANGUAGE FEATURES

1.1 Realtime Features

A program for on-line control or evaluation of a technical process has
to react rapidly on spontaneously received information of the process
or on timely results. Out of this reason it is not sufficient to arrange
and go through the various divisions of the program sequentially, that
means in timely unchanged sequence. It is of importance that the more
or less complex automation problem has to be divided into problem-
justified components of different states of urgency and that the
program structure must be fitted to this problem structure. This
causes the existence of independent program elements for sub-problems
ready to be solved timely sequentially among other problems (e.g. procedures). However, there also arise independent program elements for
sub-problems, which based on a timely not determined cause (e.g. disturbance
in the process under control) have to be solved immediately parallel to
other problems.
The execution of such a program element is called "task", for determination
of urgency such tasks can be provided with priorities.

Concerning the definition and combination of tasks - with regard to the
technical process - PEARL offers the following possibilities:

. Definition of tasks, e.g.
> SUPPLY: **TASK PRIORITY** 2;
>> taskbody (definitions, statements)
> **END;**

. Start (activation), e.g.
> **ACTIVATE** SUPPLY;

. Termination, e.g.
> **TERMINATE** PRINTING;

. Suspension, e.g.
> **SUSPEND** STATISTICS;

. Continuation, e.g.

   CONTINUE STATISTICS;

. Delay, e.g.

   AFTER 5 **SEC RESUME;**

According to demands of automation problems some of these statements
can be scheduled for their (repeated) execution, e.g. scheduled for the
case of time entrance, the end of a duration or the occurrence of an
interrupt:

WHEN READY **ACTIVATE** SUPPLY;

(Meaning: Each time when the interrupt READY occurs, the task
SUPPLY has to be activated.)

Schedules can also determine the timely periodical start:

AT 12:0:0 **EVERY** 30 **MIN UNTIL** 15:0:0 ACTIVATE PROTOCOL;

As far as certain actions do not interfere, different tasks execute their
statements independently of each other. Sometimes however synchronization
of two or more tasks is required, e.g. if a task periodically creates data
for other tasks and puts them into a buffer. In this case the producer
is not allowed to work faster than the consumer.

Synchronization problems of higher complexity arise, if a task must have
exclusive access to a file (when writing), while others also participate
simultaneously (when reading).

In order to solve such synchronization problems PEARL contains the
synchronization primitives sema and bolt variables.

1.2 Input and Output

In order to cope with devices of standard periphery (printer, card reader, disc etc.) or process periphery (measurement points, valves and so on) as well as with the administration of files PEARL provides computer independent statements.

Devices and files are being summarized with the term data station.
In general there exist two kinds of data transfer:

.   The transfer of data without transforming them to (or from) external representation:
    This kind of data transfer is provided for file handling allowing sequential and direct access and for transfer of process data.

    Examples:

        READ ARTICLE **FROM** ARTICLEFILE **BY** POS (10);
        SEND OFF **TO** MOTOR (I);

.   The transfer of data with transforming them to (or from) external representation:
    This means for example the representation of data with characters of the character set of the data station.

    Example:

        PUT RESULT **TO** PRINTER **BY** F (5) ;

The names of data stations are free-to-be-chosen. This results by dividing a PEARL program into computer dependent and mostly computer independent divisions.

1.3   Program Structure

Program systems for solving highly complex automation problems should
be modular. PEARL meets this requirement based on the fact that a
PEARL program is composed of one or several independently compilable
units, the so-called modules. In order that statements for input/output
as well as for handling events in the technical process (interrupts) or
in the computer system (signals) can be programmed computer independently, generally a module consists of a system division and a problem
division.

The hardware configuration is described in the system division. In particular,
freely-chosen user identifications may be attached to devices, interrupts,
and signals.

In the following example a valve is connected with the connection point 3
of a digital output device which has the computer-dependent "system
identification" DIGOUT(1). The valve, i.e. the connection point 3 of
DIGOUT(1), shall become the freely-chosen "user identification" VALVE.

VALVE: DIGOUT(1) * 3;

Now it is possible to program the algorithm for solving the input/output
problem computer independently in the problem division by using the
user identification introduced in the system division, e.g.:

TAKE STATUS FROM VALVE;

2. RULES FOR THE CONSTRUCTION OF PEARL PHRASES

A PEARL program can be written without usage of special program-forms; no special attention has to be paid to the fact that a statement begins on a certain line.

All elements of a PEARL program are composed of the following characters. Character string denotations and comments are permitted to be composed of each character, which is accepted by the machine configuration.

2.1 Character Set

The character set of PEARL contains the following elements:

- capital letters A - Z,
- the digits 0 to 9 and
- the special characters
  - ⌣ blank, space,
  - ' apostrophe,
  - (left parenthesis,
  -) right parenthesis,
  - , comma,
  - . period, pot,
  - ; semicolon,
  - : colon,
  - + plus sign,
  - - minus sign, hyphen,
  - * asterisk,
  - / slash,
  - = equal-sign,
  - < left angle bracket,
  - > right angle bracket,
  - [left bracket,
  -] right bracket

The following combinations of special characters are being interpreted as one unit:

**	exponentiation operator
/*	begin of a comment,
*/	end of a comment,
//	integer division operator,
==	operator equal,
/=	operator not equal,
< =	operator less or equal,
> =	operator greater or equal,
< >	operator cyclic shift,
> <	operator concatenation,
:=	assignment symbol,
<-	transfer direction symbol: arrow left,
<->	transfer direction symbol: double arrow,
->	transfer direction symbol: arrow right.

In case there aren't all of these symbols available on the device concerning program-writing, the following characters could be used alternatively:

LT	for	<
GT	for	>
NE	for	/=
LE	for	< =
GE	for	> =
CSHIFT	for	< >
CAT	for	> <
(/	for	[
/)	for	]

2.2   Basic Elements

A PEARL program is built up by the following basic elements:

- identifier
- number constant denotation
- string constant denotation
- time constant denotation
- label constant denotation
- comments
- delimiters, i.e. special characters or combinations of them.

Identifiers, number, string, time and label constant denotations must be separated from each other by comments or delimiters.

2.2.1   Identifiers

Identifiers are used to form names of objects (e.g. number variables, procedures). They consist of a sequence of capital letters and/or digits; this sequence has to start with a capital letter.

Examples: COUNTER1, DISPO

Some identifiers have a specific meaning on determined positions of PEARL programs; these identifiers are called keywords. For example BIT and GOTO are such keywords. Please find a list of all keywords as appendix; for reasons of readability they are double printed in this book.

2.2.2 Number Constant Denotations

Number constant denotations define integers and reals.
Integers can be written in decimal or in dual. If decimal-writing is
applied, an integer is written as a sequence of digits.
The dual writing of an integer consists of a sequence of digits 0 and 1,
which is ended by the letter B.

Examples:

integer	decimal	dual
6	6	110B
123	123	1111011B

Reals may be written as sequence

(i)   of one pot, one integer and optionally an exponent to basic 10,
      whereby an exponent consists of a sequence of the character E,
      optionally a plus or minus sign and an integer.

Examples: .123   (corresponds to 0.123)
           .123E2   (corresponds to 12.3)
           .123E-1   (corresponds to 0.0123)

(ii) of an integer and the sequence indicated under (i).

Example: 3.123E2   (corresponds to 312.3)

(iii) of an integer, one pot and optionally an exponent.

Example: 3.   (corresponds to 3.0)

(iv) of an integer and an exponent.

Example: 3E-2   (corresponds to 0.03)

Furthermore it is possible to define the precision of the presentation
of number constant denotations. This is done by putting into parenthesis
the number of bits just after the number constant denotation, which are
used in the computer internal representation without any pre-sign.

Example: 123(15)   The integer 123 is represented in 15 bits.

In case of no indication of precision, implicitly the precision defined in a length definition (see part III, 15) or - if also missing - an implementation dependent precision is taken, which is defined in the user manual of the specific implementation.

2.2.3 String Constant Denotations

Character string or bit string constant denotations may be introduced and used. A character string constant denotation consists of an apostrophe, a sequence of characters - free-to-be-chosen - (with the exception of apostrophe) and an apostrophe.

Example: 'GIVE INDEX: '

Should however the character string constant denotation contain an apostrophe, then two apostrophs immediately following each other have to be written.

Example: 'G''INDEX: '

A bit string constant denotation may be written using binary digits (B1), tetral digits (B2), octal digits (B3) or sedecimal digits (B4).

Form Bi (i = 1, ..., 4) consists of an apostrophe, a sequence of

.   the digits 0 to 1 in case B1
.   the digits 0 to 3 in case B2
.   the digits 0 to 7 in case B3
.   the digits 0 to 9 and letters A to F in case B4

as well as an apostrophe with corresponding indication B1 or B2 or B3 or B4.

Example: '110010100111'B1   corresponds to
                '302213'B2   corresponds to
                  '6247'B3   corresponds to
                  'CA7'B4

For application just write B instead of B1. The following tables show the arrangement between binary form and other forms:

B2	B1	B3	B1	B4	B1
0	00	0	000	0	0000
1	01	1	001	1	0001
2	10	2	010	2	0010
3	11	3	011	3	0011
		4	100	4	0100
		5	101	5	0101
		6	110	6	0110
		7	111	7	0111
				8	1000
				9	1001
				A	1010
				B	1011
				C	1100
				D	1101
				E	1110
				F	1111

2.2.4 Time Constant Denotations

Clock constant denotations and duration constant denotations may be
introduced and used.

A clock constant denotation consists of a positive integer for hour-indication, an integer between 0 and 59 for minute-indication and a real
between 0 and 59.999... for indication of seconds, divided each time
by a colon. The hour-indication is interpreted by modulo 24.

Examples:

    11:30:00   means 11.30 a.m.

    15:45:3.5   means 03.45 p.m. and 3.5 seconds

    25:00:00   means 01.00 a.m.

A duration constant denotation consists of an hour-indication, minute-
and second-indication, whereby various parts can be missing. An hour-
indication consists of an integer and the characters **HRS,** a minute-indication consists of an integer and the characters **MIN,** a second-indication
consists of an integer or real and the characters **SEC.**

Examples:

     5 **MIN** 30 **SEC**   means 5 minutes and 30 seconds

     .05 **SEC**   means 50 milli-seconds

The integers and reals used in time constant denotations are not allowed to contain a precision indication.

2.2.5 Comments

Comments serve for explanation of programs and are without significance concerning program execution. They have to be arranged between the combinations of special characters /* and */ and even could contain freely-chosen characters with the exception of the combination */ for end-of-comment.

Example: /*** DISPOSITION OF DEVICES ***/

2.3 Construction of PEARL Phrases

The PEARL admissible phrases are described in the following chapters. In order that these descriptions are exact and as compact as possible, some additional formal possibilities are needed with the verbal formulation. These formal possibilities use certain meta symbols, among other the symbols / and (and), which are also elements of the PEARL character set. In order to avoid misunderstandings these symbols are underlined in PEARL syntax rules when they indicate PEARL characters and not meta symbols. Within examples of PEARL programs they always have the meaning of PEARL characters.

Each phrase has a name; it is defined by this name with the assistance of the meta symbol ::=

    name-of-phrase ::=
        definition-of-phrase

Example:

```
letter ::=
     A  or  B  or ... or  Z
digit ::=
     0 or 1 or ... or 9
```

As this example shows the definition of a phrase may contain elements which are alternatively chosen when building-up a phrase. For abbreviation these alternatives are divided by the meta symbol / for future purposes or are stated below each other in braces.

Example:

```
letter ::=
     A / B / ... / Z
digit ::=
     ⎧ 0 ⎫
     ⎪ 1 ⎪
     ⎨ . ⎬
     ⎪ . ⎪
     ⎪ . ⎪
     ⎩ 9 ⎭
```

Should however an element be stated as often as wanted, but at least one time, it will be presented above with three pots.

Example:

```
simple-integer-constant-denotation ::=
     digit ···
```

In order to express the possibility that an element may be missing when building-up the phrase it is enclosed between the meta symbols (/ and (/ ("option-brackets").

Examples:

```
integer-constant-denotation ::=
     simple-integer-constant-denotation  (/ ( precision ) /)
```

simple-real-constant-denotation ::=

$$\left\{ \begin{array}{l} \left\{ \begin{array}{l} (/ \text{ digit}^{\cdots} /) . \text{ digit}^{\cdots} \\ \text{digit}^{\cdots} \end{array} \right\} (/ \text{ exponent-part } /) \\ \text{digit}^{\cdots} \text{ exponent-part} \end{array} \right\}$$

identifier ::=

$$\text{letter } (/ \left\{ \begin{array}{l} \text{letter} \\ \text{digit} \end{array} \right\}^{\cdots} /)$$

Two further rules were being implied here:
The definition of a phrase may again contain names of phrases. Furthermore the braces and option-brackets are also used to form new elements
from elements. Consequently the last example is equivalent to the following
example.

Example:

    identifier ::=
        letter (/ letter / digit /) $^{\cdots}$

Another kind of summarizing elements is to enclose them in parenthesis:
The rule

    character-string-denotation ::=

$$, \left\{ \begin{array}{l} \text{character-without-apostrophe} \\ \text{"} \end{array} \right\}^{\cdots} ,$$

is equivalent to the rule

    character-string-denotation ::=
        ' (character-without-apostrophe / ") $^{\cdots}$ '

Lists, whose elements are divided by a determined character (e.g. "MOTOR,
OUT, VALUE" is divided by commas) are defined as follows:
One list-element and the dividing character are stated in the definition
of the corresponding phrase whereby the dividing character is provided
above with two pots.

Example:

    identifier-list ::=
        identifier , $^{\cdots}$

14

For better understanding and/or more exact description of the definition of a phrase often elements are provided with an explaining or
restricting comment, which in turn is divided from the element by
the symbol § .

Example:

list-of-devices ::=
    identifier§device , ··

Part II

Basic Possibilities

1. PROGRAM STRUCTURE

A PEARL program consists of one or several units, so-called modules, which are compiled independently. Each module consists of a system division and/or a problem division.

The system division displays those interrupts, signals and devices of the peripheral environment (process and standard periphery) which are used in the PEARL program. The programmer has to attach freely chosen names to all interrupts, signals and devices of the system division in order to refer to these (computer independent) names within the realtime and input/output statements of the problem division.

The algorithm for solving the given automation problem is described in the problem division by defining

- problem data
  (integers, reals, bit strings, character strings, durations, clocks)

- control data for handling sequential activities
  (labels, procedures for repeatedly appearing sub problems)

- control data for handling parallel activities
  (tasks for simultaneously solving of sub problems, interrupts, signals and synchronization objects) and

- control data for input and output
  (data stations, formats).

The necessary statements are stated in procedures and tasks - together with further "local" definitions only needed there. Generally data are only allowed to be used (within statements) after their definition. Data defined on module level, that means not defined within procedures and tasks, may be used within all procedures and tasks of the corresponding module.

The general form of a module is:

module ::=
    MODULE (/ (identifier§of-the-module) /);
        $\left\{ \begin{array}{l} \text{system-division (/ problem division /)} \\ \text{problem division} \end{array} \right\}$
    MODEND;

system-division ::=
    SYSTEM; (/ connection ⋯ /)

problem-division ::=
    PROBLEM; (/ definition ⋯ /)

Example:

    MODULE;
    SYSTEM;
        Description of connections and introduction of names for
        periphery elements

    PROBLEM;
        $\left. \begin{array}{l} \text{Definition of problem data} \\ \text{Definition of interrupts} \end{array} \right\}$ on module level

        Definition of a task
            Definition of local problem data
            Statements

        Definition of a procedure
            Definition of local problem data
            Definition of local procedures
            Statements

            . . .

    MODEND;

18

Within procedures and tasks no control-data for handling parallel
activities or input/output can be defined.

The first (from outside) started task causes the start of the other tasks
and procedures and/or the planning of starts of other tasks, e.g. in
case of occurrence of an interrupt. The user manual has to define in
detail the start procedure. Concerning the implementations of Werum,
the task named START is started automatically by the PEARL system
after having loaded the PEARL program.

Connections between modules can be made by global objects (see part III, 6).

2. PROBLEM DATA

When being executed a PEARL program uses and changes among other objects integers, reals, bit strings, character strings, clocks and durations. These problem data occur in form of constants or as values of variables. Constants identify themselves by their writing (see part I, 2.2) and maintain their value during the complete execution of the program. Variables refer to data (their values), which can change during the execution of the program.

The range of a variable generally concentrates on one kind of data, e.g. bit strings, determining the type of this variable. (Bit string variables only have bit strings as values.) This type has to be determined by the declaration of a variable together with its identifier.

Example:

Declaration of a variable X of the type real.
DECLARE X FLOAT;

Variables are declared on module level, in procedures or in tasks. On module level declared variables are known throughout the whole module; each task and procedure of the module can use them within expressions or change their values in assignments by indication of their identifiers. A variable declared in a task or procedure is only known within its corresponding task or procedure and can only be used and changed there.

On module level or in a procedure or in a task a variable is only permitted to be declared one time. In case an identifier X is declared as variable on module level as well as in a procedure or a task, two different variables are introduced: In this corresponding procedure or task X refers to the variable (locally) declared in the procedure or task; outside of the procedure or task X refers to the variable declared on module level (see part III/5 for details).

Example:

```
PROBLEM;
        DECLARE X FLOAT;        1st declaration on module level
        DECLARE X FIXED;        2nd declaration on module level (wrong)

P:  PROCEDURE;
        DECLARE X FIXED;        Declaration in procedure P (allowed)
        . . .
        X := 3;                 Assignment to local variable
        . . .
        END;

T:  TASK;
        . . .
        X := 5;                 Assignment to the variable X declared
        . . .                   on module level
        END;
. . .
```

A variable refers to one data element, e.g. one integer, one bit string, etc.; such scalar variables are explained in the following paragraphs. The possibilities of summarizing such scalar variables to arrays and structures are described in II/2.2 and III/1.

2.1 Scalar Problem Data

When declaring a variable its type has to be indicated in a type (or mode) attribute. If one has to declare different variables of the same type this may be done in form of a list within one declaration:

DECLARE (X, Y, Z) FLOAT;

These three variables X, Y and Z are declared with the type attribute FLOAT. For easier writing it is allowed to combine various declarations to one declaration - just by simply dividing them by a comma:

DECLARE X FLOAT, I FIXED;

21

In general variables for scalar problem data can be declared as follows:

declaration-of-scalar-problem-data ::=
    (DECLARE / DCL)
    (one-identifier-or-list simple-mode) , ";

one-identifier-or-list ::=
    identifier / (identifier , ")

simple-mode ::=
    type-integer / type-real / type-bit-string /
    type-character-string / type-clock / type-duration

2.1.1 Variables for Integers

Variables for integers (see I/2.2.2) are being declared with the type
attribute **FIXED**.

type-integer ::=
    FIXED   (/ (precision) /)

precision ::=
    simple-integer-constant-denotation

The precision indicates the number of bits used to represent the value
of the variable (without pre-sign). In case the precision indication is
missing, the precision defined in a length definition (see III/15) is used.
If in addition the length definition is missing, an implementation
dependent precision is used, which is defined in the user manual.

Example:

DCL   RESULT FIXED (31),
        (I, J, K) FIXED;
    . . .
I := 2;

2.1.2 Values for Reals

Variables of type real (with integers or reals (see I/2.2.2) as values) are declared with the type attribute **FLOAT**:

    type-real ::=
        FLOAT (/ (precision) /)

The same rule applies as in 2.1.1.

Example:

    DCL (X, Y, Z) **FLOAT**, COEFF **FLOAT** (31);
    . . .
    X := 3.5; Y := 1;

2.1.3 Variables for Bit Strings

Variables for bit strings (see I/2.2.3) are to be declared with the type attribute **BIT** .

    type-bit-string ::=
        BIT (/ (length) /)

    length ::=
        simple-integer-constant-denotation

Length indicates the number of elements of the bit string. In case the length indication is missing, it either has to be defined in a length definition (see III/15) or it is used as length 1.

Example:

    DCL XCOORD **BIT** (2), YCOORD **BIT** (8);
    . . .
    XCOORD := '01'B; YCOORD := 'A9'B4;

2.1.4 Variables for Character Strings

Variables for character strings (see I/2.2.5) are declared with the type attribute **CHARACTER.**

> type-character-string ::=
> (**CHARACTER** / **CHAR**) (/ (length) /)

Length stands for the number of characters. In case the length indication is missing, it either has to be defined in a length definition (see III/ 15) or length 1 is used.

Example:

> **DCL** IDENTIFICATION CHAR (6);
> . . .
> IDENTIFICATION := 'BCD/27';

2.1.5 Variables for Clocks

Variables for clocks (see I/2.2.4) are to be declared with the type attribute **CLOCK.**

> type-clock ::=
> **CLOCK**

Example:

> **DCL** TIME **CLOCK**;
> . . .
> TIME := 12:30:00;

2.1.6 Variables for Durations

Variables for durations (see I/2.2.4) have to be declared with the type attribute **DURATION.**

type-duration ::=

    DURATION / DUR

Example:

  DCL DELAY **DUR;**

  . . .

  DELAY := 0.1 SEC;

2.2 Arrays of Problem Data

If possible, programmers try to summarize objects of the same kind under
one identifier and to refer to the various objects by using this identifier
and an index.

Example:

An intelligent device IC controls three other devices D(1), D(2) and
D(3). At output of bit string '0001'B to IC, it shall switch on D(1),
at output of '0010'B it shall switch on D(2), and at output of
'0100'B it shall switch on D(3). Here the possibility of summarizing
the three turn-on-signals to one identifier (e.g. DEVICEON) is   given,
and to address a single signal by index:

  DCL DEVICEON (1:3) **BIT**(4), I **FIXED;**

  . . .

  DEVICEON (1) := '0001'B;

  DEVICEON (2) := '0010'B;

  DEVICEON (3) := '0100'B;

  . . .

Transfer of the value of I (index of device to be switched on) from
another program part.

Output of DEVICEON (I) to the intelligent device.

In general scalar problem data of the same type can be summarized to
n-dimensional arrays (n = 1,2,3, ...). At its declaration the array is given
an identifier, the various elements of the array (scalar variables)

25

are being addressed with this identifier and with indication of their position (index) within this array.

Example:

    DCL TABLE (1:2, 0:3) **FIXED**;

A 2-dimensional array is declared, whereby the first dimension possesses the lower bound 1 and the upper bound 2, that means - it possesses length 2, while the second dimension has the lower bound 0 and the upper bound 3, that means it has length 4. This signifies, that TABLE consists of 8 scalar **FIXED**-variables

TABLE (1,0)   TABLE (1,1)   TABLE (1,2)   TABLE (1,3)
TABLE (2,0)   TABLE (2,1)   TABLE (2,2)   TABLE (2,3)

Generally an array of problem data has to be declared as follows:

declaration-of-arrays-of-problem-data ::=
    (DECLARE / DCL)
    (one-identifier-or-list bound-list simple-type-attribute), ";

bound-list ::=
    (((/(/ - /) simple-integer-constant-denotation§lower-bound : /)
        (/ - /) simple-integer-constant-denotation§upper-bound
    ), ")

Corresponding to this also negative integers are allowed as dimension bounds. The upper bound of a dimension must - by all means - always be larger or must be equal to its lower bound.

If the lower bound is not indicated, then the value 1 will be used.

Example:

    DCL DEVICEON (3) **BIT** (4),
        TABLE (2, 0:3) **FIXED**,
        MESSAGE (20) **CHAR** (12);

The one-dimensional array MESSAGE may contain 20 error-messages; in the case of error i MESSAGE (i) can be put out to a terminal (i = 1, ..., 20).

Arrays may be declared together with scalar variables in one declaration, e.g.

```
DCL  MESSAGE (20) CHAR (12),
     (I, J, K) FIXED,
     (DEVICEON, DEVICEOFF) (3) BIT (4);
```

Please find described in paragraph 2 of the appendix, which objects may be summarized to arrays in general.

3. PROCEDURES

When implementing a process automation, structured programming suggests that each logically independent algorithm corresponds to an independent section of the program, which is given a name, particularly when the algorithm requires execution at several points in the complete program, with perhaps only a change in its arguments (parameters). The execution of such a program section is initiated by calling it by name and providing it with any actual parameters required.

If the call is required to have the same effect as had the program section been carried out in its place, then the section is declared and started in PEARL as a procedure. Otherwise - when the statements following the call are to be carried out parallel to it - the section is declared and started as a task. Tasks are dealt with in section 4 (parallel activities).

Procedures which return a result are called function procedures, all others are called subroutine procedures.

Example of a subroutine procedure:

The procedure OUTPUT converts the positioning information POSITION of type FIXED to a bit string and outputs it to the device to be positioned, which is indicated by the number MACHNO of type FIXED. The task CONTROL (among others) calls OUTPUT.

```
PROBLEM;
 . . .
OUTPUT: PROCEDURE ( ( POSITION, MACHNO ) FIXED (15) );
    DCL BINPOS BIT (8) ;
        Conversion of POSITION to BINPOS
        Output of BINPOS to the machine MACHNO
    END;  /* DECLARATION OF OUTPUT */

CONTROL: TASK;
    DCL (POS /* ACTUAL POSITION REQUIRED */,
        NO  /*  MACHINE NUMBER */ ) FIXED (15) ;

    . . .

    Assignments to POS and NO
    CALL OUTPUT (POS, NO);

    . . .

    END; /* DECLARATION OF CONTROL */
 . . .
```

POSITION and MACHNO are the formal parameters of OUTPUT, POS and NO are actual parameters. BINPOS is a local variable in OUTPUT which is only known within OUTPUT.

Example of a function procedure:

The procedure NEXTMACHINE determines by means of the reservation plan RESPLAN the machine number of that one of all available machines which is next to be engaged. RESPLAN is not to be passed as parameter and the result is returned as a number of type **FIXED**. NEXTMACHINE must be declared and called within the task SUPPLY.

```
PROBLEM;
    DCL RESPLAN ... ;
    SUPPLY: TASK;
        DCL MACHNO FIXED (15) ;
        . . .
        NEXTMACHINE: PROCEDURE RETURNS ( FIXED (15) );
            DCL NO FIXED (15) ; /* NO OF NEXT MACHINE */
                determination of NO using RESPLAN
            RETURN (NO);
            END; /* DECLARATION OF NEXTMACHINE */
        . . .
        MACHNO := NEXTMACHINE;
        . . .
        END; /* DECLARATION OF SUPPLY */
    . . .
```

Since the variable RESPLAN is declared at module level it can be used and where necessary changed by all the procedures and tasks in the module.

3.1   Declaration of Procedures

The series of statements which is to be executed in place of a procedure
call is laid down in a procedure declaration under a procedure name.
The statements in the procedure may use problem or control data

. which are defined at module level or in an enclosing scope (see III/5)

. which are specified as formal parameters, i.e. in place of the actual
  expressions or variables which are passed as actual parameters when
  the procedure is called

. or which are defined locally within the procedure.

The local declarations and the statements of the procedure form the
procedure body.

```
procedure-declaration ::=
    identifier :    (PROCEDURE / PROC)
                    (/ list-of-formal-parameters /)
                    (/ result-attribute /)
                    (/ resident-attribute /)
                    (/ reentrant-attribute /)
                    (/ global-attribute /) ;
                    procedure-body
                    END;

procedure-body ::=
    (/ declaration ··· /) (/ statement ··· /)

list-of-formal-parameters ::=
    (( one-identifier-or-list  (/ virt-bound-list /)
        parameter-mode (/ IDENT / IDENTICAL /) ), ·· )

virt-bound-list ::=
    (( / , ··· / ) )

parameter-mode ::=
    simple-mode / complex-parameter-mode

result-attribute ::=
    RETURNS ( simple-mode / structure-mode / reference-mode )
```

30

Resident-attribute, reentrant-attribute, global-attribute, structure-mode
and reference-mode are handled in sections 9, 10, 6, 1 and 4 of part III,
complex-parameter-mode is explained by means of a list under point 2
of the appendix.

Subroutine procedures are declared without and function procedures
with a result attribute. Its mode determines the type of the result which
is returned at the point of call. This return is effected by means of the
return statement in the form:

RETURN (expression);

The value of the expression must have the type specified in the result-
attribute.

The execution of the procedure body of a function procedure is terminated
by carrying out a return statement. Function procedures may not be
left in any other way.

The execution of a subroutine procedure is terminated by

. executing a return statement in the form

RETURN;

. or by executing the last statement of the procedure body.

A procedure body may contain declarations, e.g. the declarations of
local problem data which are then known only within the procedure body.
In addition, so-called 'nested procedures' may be declared. The question
of the uniqueness of names, which also arises when procedures are declared within tasks, is dealt with in part III/5 in connection with blocks.

The procedure call establishes a correspondence between the actual
parameters given in the call and the formal parameters specified in the
procedure. This occurs for each parameter in one of two ways, depending
whether the formal parameter has the attribute **IDENTICAL** or not.
Both ways are explained in the next paragraph.

31

The number of commas (n) in a virtual bounds list specifies that the parameter is an (n+1)-dimensional array. For example, if the one-dimensional array "A (10) **FIXED**" is to be passed to a procedure P whose formal parameter is B then B must be specified: "B ( ) **FIXED**".

3.2   Calling Procedures

Subroutine procedures are called by means of the keyword **CALL** :

    call-statement ::=
        CALL identifier§subroutine-procedure (/ list-of-actual-parameters /) ;

    list-of-actual-parameters ::=
        (expression, ··)

Example:

    . . .
    assignment to POS and NO
    CALL OUTPUT (POS, NO);

The call-statement has the effect that the stated actual parameters are associated, in the order they are written, with the formal parameters of the called procedure; then the procedure body is executed. Subsequently those statements following the procedure call are executed.

A function procedure is never called directly but only within an expression, by giving its name and actual parameters:

    function-call ::=
        identifier§function-procedure (/ list-of-actual-parameters /)

Example:

    The function procedure ARI evaluates the arithmetic mean of an array of N **FLOAT** variables. This mean is then printed together with the text 'ARITHM MEAN'.

```
ARI: PROC ( ARRAY ( )FLOAT, N FIXED ) RETURNS (FLOAT);
    DCL SUM FLOAT;
    SUM := 0;
    FOR I FROM 1 BY 1 TO N REPEAT
        SUM := SUM + ARRAY (I);
    END;
    RETURN (SUM / N);
    END; /* ARI */

    DCL VALUE (10) FLOAT;
    . . .
        input of values
    PUT ARI (READING , 10), 'ARITHM MEAN' TO PRINTER BY LIST;
    . . .
```

In the evaluation of a function call the given actual parameters are associated
with the formal parameters of the function procedure in the order they are
written, and the procedure body is then executed. Thereafter the evaluation
of the expression or statement which contains the function call is continued
– in the above example the evaluation of the expression 'ARITHM MEAN'
in the PUT statement.

The type of an actual parameter in a call statement or in a function call
must agree with that of the corresponding formal parameter.

The assignment of the actual parameters to the formal parameters may
be carried out in one of two ways: When the specification of the formal
parameters carries the attribute IDENTICAL or IDENT, the assignment
is effected by means of identification, otherwise by value transfer.
In the value transfer case, also called "call by value", a new variable
local to the procedure body is declared, with the type of the formal parameter, i.e. the formal parameter becomes a local variable of the given
type. The value of the actual parameter is then transferred to this variable.
Thus an assignment to the formal parameter by a statement in the procedure body hasn't any effect on the actual parameter. In addition an actual
parameter may in this case be any expression.
In the case of identification, also called "call by reference", a formal
parameter is identified with the corresponding actual parameter - i.e.
the value of the actual parameter is accessed in the procedure body

under the name of the formal parameter. Thus an assignment to a formal
parameter has in this case the effect of an assignment to that variable
which has been passed as actual parameter. Therefore in this case only
names (of problem and control data) and not expressions may be passed
as actual parameters.

Example:

```
PROBLEM;
    P1: PROC ( PI FIXED, PJ FIXED IDENT, PX FLOAT );
        . . .
        PI := 3;
        PJ := 5;
        END;  /* P1 */

    P2: PROC . . .;
        DCL (I, J) FIXED, A(100) FLOAT;
        . . .
        I := 2;  J := 4;  A(I) := 2.5;
        CALL P1 (I, J, 3*A(I) - 1);
        . . .
        END; /* P2 */
    . . .
```

After the call of P1 in P2, I still has the value 2, while J has the
value 5.

As shown by the syntax rule for procedure declaration (see 3.1), the values
of actual parameters may be of the types:

.   integer
.   real
.   bit string
.   character string
.   clock
.   duration.

There are also more complex types permitted which are described in
part III. All permissible parameter types are listed in the second section
of the appendix.

34

4.   PARALLEL ACTIVITIES

A typical process control application consists of

-   asynchronous, i.e. independent concurrent execution of routines
    (processes) which may be started at pre-determined times or in
    answer to external events, and

-   synchronization of such processes at specified points, e.g. for the
    exchange of data.

Such operations are programmed in PEARL by means of tasks, interrupts and synchronization variables.

A task is the execution of a piece of a program under the control of
the operating system. This piece, the body of the task, consists, as does
a procedure, of PEARL definitions and statements. Before execution
a task must be declared; it is thereby allotted an identifier by means of
which it can later be influenced, e.g. started or delayed.
Since the tasks of one program will normally have only one available
processor they will compete for it as well as for other resources such
as shared peripherals. The operating system has to apportion access to
these resources according to the urgency of the tasks. To facilitate this
a task may be assigned a positive integer as priority, there lower numbers
indicate greater priority. The specified priorities are used by the system
to govern the use of resources: for example, when a task having access
to the processor requests use of another facility which is already occupied,
the system will pass access of the processor to that waiting task which
has the highest priority.
Similarly, a priority-governed transfer of processor access will take
place each time a system function is called - e.g. on an interrupt, when
carrying out a task control instruction, a synchronization, input/output
etc.

4.1   Task Declarations

The declaration of a task is carried out as for a procedure.
However, unlike procedures, tasks may only be declared at module
level, i.e. they may not be declared within the body of a procedure or
task. In addition, parameters are not permitted. However, as all the
PEARL objects at module level may be used or (where possible) amended
within the body of a task, information can be passed between tasks by
means of data at module level or by means of I/O instructions. In particular the access of several tasks to the same data must be carefully
synchronized, as described in paragraph 4.4.

Example:

A task LOG transfers a text to the variable TEXT, which must be
transmitted to a terminal by the task OUTPUT. (The necessary
synchronization instructions are described in paragraf i '.)

PROBLEM;

    DCL TEXT **CHAR** (60);

    LOG: **TASK;**

        determination of the text

        transfer to TEXT

        . . .

        END;

    OUTPUT: **TASK;**

        output of the value of TEXT

        . . .

        END;

    . . .

The general form of a task declaration is as follows:

task-declaration ::=

    identifier : **TASK** (/ priority /)

    (/ resident-attribute /) (/ global-attribute /) ;

    task-body

    END;

priority ::=

    (**PRIORITY** / **PRIO**) integer-constant-denotation

task-body ::=

    (/ declaration ··· /) (/ statement ··· /)

Resident- and global-attributes are explained in part III, sections 9 and 6.

4.2   Interrupts

An interrupt is a message, via an interrupt line, from the process under
control to the operating system, which then causes the corresponding
programmed response, e.g. "On receipt of the interrupt FINISHED,
start the task SUPPLY".
The available interrupts in a computer system are described in the
user manual, together with their system names. Those interrupts
required for a PEARL program are declared in the system division,
where user names may be assigned to them.
They are then specified under these names in the problem division so
that they may be used in task control statements (see 4.3) and interrupt statements (see part III, 12).

Example:

```
MODULE;
SYSTEM;
FINISHED: INT * 7;   /* INT * 7 is the system name */

PROBLEM;
SPECIFY FINISHED INTERRUPT;
. . .
START : TASK ;
        . . .
        WHEN FINISHED ACTIVATE SUPPLY;
        . . .
        END;
. . .
SUPPLY: TASK PRIORITY 2;
            task-body
        END;
. . .
```

37

The general form of an interrupt specification is:

interrupt-specification ::=
        (SPECIFY / SPC) one-identifier-or-list (/ ( ) /)
        (INTERRUPT / IRPT) (/ resident-attribute /) (/ global-attribute /);

The resident- and global-attributes are explained in sections 9 and 6 of part III.

It is possible to specify one-dimensional arrays of interrupts; how to declare them correspondingly within the system division is described in paragraph 7.1.

4.3   Task Control Statements

4.3.1 Schedules

A task can be started, finished, suspended, continued, delayed and pre-vented from being started or continued.
The statements for control of the sequential flow of programs (e.g. jumps, loops, procedure-calls) are completely executed after their evaluation; that means, if such a statement is executed, it has no further effects. Contrary to this the execution of a statement concerning the start of a task can result in a multifold start of this task.
When and how many times a task statement shall be executed, is determined by its schedule, i.e. the set of conditions that are set up in a task control statement:

        task-control-statement ::=
            (/ schedule /) task-statement

Only if the conditions expressed by the schedule are met, the task-statement is executed. (When executing the task-control-statement, the execution of the task-statement is scheduled for the time, when the conditions of the schedule are met.)

In case no schedule is given, the task-statement shall be executed immediately, but only one time.

Example:

> **ACTIVATE** STATISTICS;
>> means, that the task STATISTICS shall be started immediately.

> **AT** 20:0:0 **ACTIVATE** STATISTICS;
>> means however, that the task STATISTICS shall be started
>> not before 8 p.m.

The first execution of a task-statement with schedule may take place
at a certain time, after a certain duration or at the occurrence of a
certain interrupt or immediately.

> schedule ::=
> $\left\{\begin{array}{l}\textbf{AT}\ \text{expression§time}\ (/\ \text{frequence}\ /)\\ \textbf{AFTER}\ \text{expression§duration}\ (/\ \text{frequence}\ /)\\ \textbf{WHEN}\ \text{name§interrupt}\ (/\ \textbf{AFTER}\ \text{expression§duration}\ /)\ (/\ \text{frequence}\ /)\\ \text{frequence}\end{array}\right\}$

> frequence ::=
>> **ALL** expression§duration
>> (/ (**UNTIL** expression§time) / (**DURING** expression§duration) /)

The notion " **AT** expression§time " determines the time of the first execution
of the task-statement, " **AFTER** expression§duration " determines the
length of the time interval between the execution of the task-control-
statement and the first execution of the task-statement. The notion " **WHEN**
name§interrupt" determines that the task-statement shall be executed for the
first time, when the specified interrupt occurs, the optional addition
" **AFTER** expression§duration " determines that the task-statement shall be
executed for the first time x time-units after the occurrence of the specified
interrupt where x corresponds to the specified expression§duration.
If **AT, AFTER** and **WHEN** are missing, the task-statement shall be executed immediately.

In case the task-statement shall be repeated periodically after its first
execution then the duration for the period has to be determined by " **ALL**
expression§duration".

In order to finish the periodic execution a certain time (UNTIL expression§time) or a certain duration (DURING expression§duration) may be determined for the last execution of the task-statement.

Contrary to the other schedules the schedule " WHEN name§interrupt ... " remains valid after the condition is met, i.e. when the specified interrupt occurs, the execution of the task-statement is again scheduled for the next occurrence of that interrupt (keeping all optional additions of the old schedule). The old schedule itself becomes invalid; an old frequence is cancelled.

In case the schedule " WHEN ... " shall be valid for all elements of an interrupt-array, only the identifier of the array has to be specified (see III/12).

A schedule gets valid when executing the task-control-statement which contains the schedule. (Now the execution of the corresponding task-statement is scheduled.) The expressions of the schedule and the task-statement are evaluated therein.

The schedule gets invalid (that means the corresponding task-statement will not be executed),

. if it starts with AFTER or ALL and the condition is met which is set-up by UNTIL or DURING or if it has the form " AFTER§duration" and the indicated duration (since the execution of the schedule) has already passed-by,

. at execution of a prevent-statement (see 4.3.7),

. at execution of a new task-control-statement, which contains the same task-statement as the previous one. The presiously stated schedule is in turn replaced by the new one, or in case no new one is given, the previously stated schedule is eliminated.

Example:

. . .

AT 12:0:0 ACTIVATE PROTOCOL;
ALL 2 HRS ACTIVATE PROTOCOL;

. . .

These two schedules can't be valid at the same time: In this case the schedule " ALL 2 HRS " replaces the schedule " AT 12:0:0" with the only exception - namely that the execution of the second statement starts after 12.00 a.m.

4.3.2 Start

The following picture reflects the possibilities to start a task directly or under consideration of different schedules.

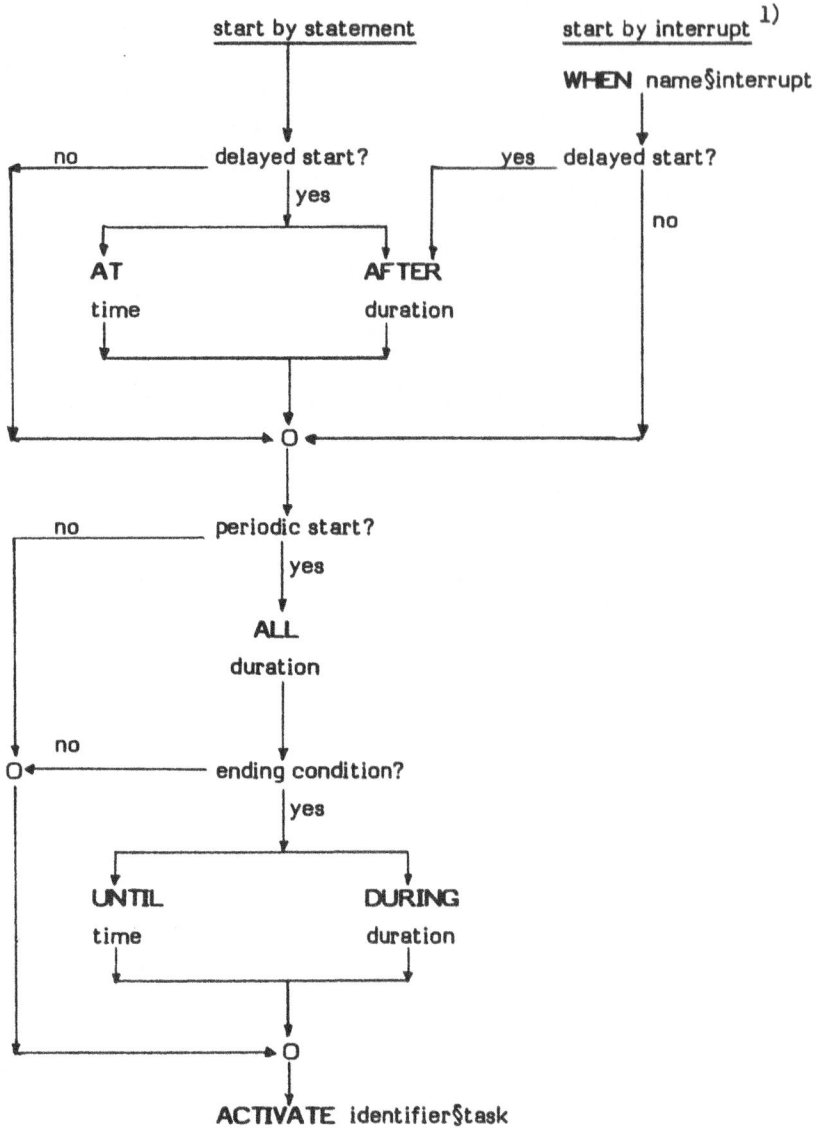

start by statement   start by interrupt [1]

WHEN name§interrupt

no   delayed start?   yes delayed start?

yes   no

AT   AFTER

time   duration

no   periodic start?

yes

ALL

duration

no   ending condition?

yes

UNTIL   DURING

time   duration

ACTIVATE identifier§task

[1] After the occurrence of an interrupt the task-statement is newly scheduled under consideration of the corresponding schedule. The old schedule gets invalid.

42

The general rule for starting a task is:

    activate-statement ::=
        (/ schedule /) **ACTIVATE** identifier§task (/ priority /) ;

At the execution of such an activate-statement, the specified task applies either immediately (without schedule) for a processor or at the specified time determined by the schedule. This task competes with all other tasks, which apply at that time for the processor. Concerning an immediate start, the task - being started - competes especially with the task starting it, if only one processor is at disposal.

The possibility exists that the specified task has already been started and isn't yet finished at the time of execution of the activate-statement. If in this case no schedule is given, then an error message is the result of it. If however, the activate-statement contains a schedule, then the specified task is continued and its renewed start is buffered with the assistance of the schedule, whereby a possibly existing schedule gets invalid.

A possibly stated priority devaluates the priority given in the declaration of this task.

A task is finished,

.   if it reaches the final **END**-statement of its body,

.   by execution of a terminate-statement for this task (see 4.3.3).

Example:

    The task TAKEPRESSURE should measure all 5 seconds the pressure
    in a boiler and should forward this information to task MONITOR .
    In case the pressure rises too rapidly, the measuring shall be repeated
    each second with higher priority. MONITOR is started by the task
    START .

```
PROBLEM;
START : TASK;
    ACTIVATE MONITOR ;
        further initializations

    END;

MONITOR : TASK PRIORITY 6 ;
    ALL 5 SEC ACTIVATE TAKEPRESSURE ;
        evaluation of measured values
        in case the pressure rises:
    ALL 1 SEC ACTIVATE TAKEPRESSURE PRIO 2;
    . . .
    END;

TAKEPRESSURE : TASK PRIO 5;
        taking pressure values from the boiler
        transfer to MONITOR
    END;
    . . .
```

4.3.3 Termination

The previous termination of a task is reached by the following statement:

terminate-statement ::=
    TERMINATE (/ identifier§task /) ;

In case the notion identifier§task is missing, then the statement refers
to the executing task (i.e. the task containing that terminate-statement
in its body is terminated).

The terminated task is deprived of all its previous resources (including
processor).
Possibly buffered activations (of existing schedules) remain valid.

4.3.4 Suspend Statement

By performing the statement

suspend-statement ::=
   SUSPEND (/ identifier§task /);

the determined task or the executing task is suspended. The task looses
its processor, this however doesn't apply to the other resources.

A suspended task can only be continued by execution of a continue
statement for this task by another task.

4.3.5 Continue Statement

A suspended task can by means of the following statement be continued
immediately, or at a specific time, or after a determined duration or
when an interrupt occurs.

continue-statement ::=
   (/ simple-schedule /)
   CONTINUE ((identifier§task (/ priority /)) / priority);

simple-schedule ::=
   (**AT** expression§time) / (**AFTER** expression§duration) /
   (**WHEN** name§interrupt)

In case identifier§task is stated, then the specified task immediately
applies for its corresponding processor - or at a time fixed in the schedule. This might possibly be done with a newly stated priority, which in
turn replaces the priority determined in the declaration or activation.

The form without identifier§task results to the fact that the executing
task applies newly for a processor at the time fixed in the schedule,
possibly even with intensified priority, which in turn replaces the previously determined priority.

45

Example:

The measuring task MEASURE should perform an output to a device;
after this it should wait for the interrupt GOON and continue with
higher priority.

MEASURE: **TASK PRIO** 8;
          measurement
   WHEN GOON **CONTINUE PRIO** 5;
         output
   SUSPEND;
         measurement with higher priority
   END;

4.3.6 Delay

The following statement allows to delay a task for a certain time or
for a certain duration or until the occurrence of a certain interrupt:

   resume-statement ::=
      simple-schedule **RESUME** ;

This statement is equivalent to the not-interruptable combination of
the statements:

   simple-schedule **CONTINUE** ;
   SUSPEND ;

After execution of the resume-statement the schedule gets invalid.

Example:

The task MONITOR is supposed to turn-on a device and to
check 10 seconds later, if it works as anticipated.

MONITOR : **TASK** ;
       turning-on of device
       AFTER 10 SEC **RESUME** ;
       testing the functions of the device
       . . .
       END ;

4.3.7 Prevent Statement

The possibility might come up of preventing the activation or continuation
of a task, that means, that its schedules are to become invalid. This
can be reached by means of the following statement:

    prevent-statement ::=
        PREVENT (/ identifier§task /) ;

This statement doesn't terminate the specified task; if identifier§task
is not mentioned, the statement refers to the executing task.

Example:

The procedure MONITOR - called by a higher related task -   commands
"Go" to a stacker crane under control, which in turn has to give
the message READY within a duration of 2 minutes - starting the
task SUPPLY. If the message READY is not received after a period
of 2 minutes, then the task TROUBLE shall be started and the
eventually possible but delayed start of SUPPLY shall be prevented.
Generally READY is received within 2 minutes and consequently
the start of TROUBLE has to be prevented.

PROBLEM;

SPECIFY READY **INTERRUPT** ;

MONITOR : **PROC** ((X , Y) **FIXED** /* COORDINATES */);
        conversion of X and Y to a bit string
        output to stacker crane

        WHEN READY **ACTIVATE** SUPPLY ;
        AFTER 2 **MIN ACTIVATE** TROUBLE ;
        . . .
        END;

SUPPLY: **TASK PRIO** 3;
        PREVENT TROUBLE ;
        . . .
        END;

TROUBLE: **TASK PRIO** 2;
        PREVENT SUPPLY ;
        . . .
        END ;

4.4 Synchronization of Tasks

Generally tasks execute their bodies independently of each other. However; it is possible that several tasks are solving parts of a highly complex problem, using commonly specific resources, especially data.

Example:

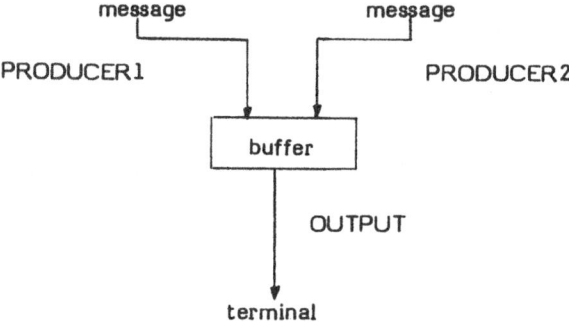

The tasks PRODUCER1 and PRODUCER2 produce data to be stored in one commonly used buffer. The task OUTPUT takes one message from the buffer and outputs it to the terminal in a certain format.

In order to enable a correct flow of operations, they have to be co-ordinated as follows:

.   OUTPUT works only in the case, when a message was buffered that means that OUTPUT is possibly waiting for further feeding by PRODUCER1 or PRODUCER2.

.   PRODUCER1 and PRODUCER2 can only buffer a message if no previously buffered message is put out by OUTPUT, that means that they possibly have to be delayed until a complete message is put out by OUTPUT.

.   Those parts of PRODUCER1 and PRODUCER2 which buffer a message have to be executed mutually exclusive.

In order to control such a co-ordination two types of synchronization variables (synchronizers) called sema and bolt variables are introduced. If the access to common resources (e.g. data, procedures and devices) should be co-ordinated, then a synchronization variable is attached to each resource. Before usage of such a resource the tasks execute a statement blocking the synchronizer and after usage they execute a statement setting free the synchronizer, which is attached to this resource.

The attachment of synchronizers to resources doesn't result by PEARL-statements, however, it is of utmost importance that a certain synchronizer is used only in connection with one specific resource.
Such an attachment is not restricted to data, procedures, devices, etc.
It might also be applicable concerning parts of programs, which all have to be finished before another program part is further executed.

4.4.1 Exclusive Synchronization by means of Sema Variables

The values of sema variables are not negative integers representing the states "released" and "requested". Zero stands for "requested", a positive integer n stands for "released".
These values can only be changed by special request and release statements.

Sema variables are declared as follows:

    DCL one-identifier-or-list SEMA ;

Example:

    DCL (ON , OFF) SEMA ;

After its declaration the sema variable is in the state "requested".

For explicitly decreasing the value of a sema variable, the following request statement has to be applied:

    REQUEST identifier§sema ;

However, the effect of this statement depends on the actual value of the corresponding sema variable:

.   In case its value is greater than zero, it will be decreased by 1.
     (Note: Execution of a request statement doesn't always put a sema variable into the state "requested".)

.   In case the value equals to zero, it remains unchanged, the executing task is suspended and is put into a waiting queue, which is attached internally to the sema variable.

The execution of the release statement

RELEASE identifier§sema;

results to the fact that the value of the identified sema variable is increased by 1. Furthermore the tasks queued by this sema variable are set free; they repeat their request statements in the sequence of priority.

Example:

The following means are to solve the known problem of buffering messages:
For input to the buffer the sema variable INTOBUFFER is used, concerning the output from the buffer the sema variable FROMBUFFER is used. INTOBUFFER and FROMBUFFER are initialized implicitly in their declarations with the state "requested". The task OUTPUT is started from outside. Before OUTPUT starts the tasks PRODUCER1 and PRODUCER2, the sema variable INTOBUFFER must get the status "released".

```
PROBLEM ;
DCL ( INTOBUFFER, FROMBUFFER ) SEMA ;

OUTPUT: TASK ;
    RELEASE INTOBUFFER ;
    ACTIVATE PRODUCER1 ;
    ACTIVATE PRODUCER2 ;
    REPEAT
        REQUEST FROMBUFFER ;
        output to the terminal
        RELEASE INTOBUFFER ;
    END ;  /* LOOP */
    END ;  /* TASK OUTPUT */

PRODUCER1: TASK ;
    REPEAT
        preparation of the message
        REQUEST INTOBUFFER ;
        buffering
        RELEASE FROMBUFFER ;
    END ;  /* LOOP */
    END ;  /* TASK PRODUCER1 */
```

PRODUCER2: **TASK** ;
    REPEAT
        preparation of the message
        REQUEST INTOBUFFER ;
        buffering
        RELEASE FROMBUFFER ;
    END ; /* LOOP */
    END ; /* TASK PRODUCER2 */

Explanation:

OUTPUT waits until FROMBUFFER is released i.e. until buffering
of an information, because FROMBUFFER can only be released
by PRODUCER1 and PRODUCER2. After output OUTPUT re-
leases INTOBUFFER , i.e. enables buffering and awaits a new message.
PRODUCER1 and PRODUCER2 can only buffer an information
if INTOBUFFER has the state "released".
After buffering of message FROMBUFFER is released, i.e. OUTPUT
is continued.

Based on incorrect synchronizations tasks might constantly suspend themselves. Such deadlocks might possibly be caused by the following program
organization:

Task T1	Task T2
REQUEST S1;	**REQUEST** S2;
1. region	1. region
REQUEST S2;	**REQUEST** S1;
2. region	2. region
RELEASE S2;	**RELEASE** S1;
RELEASE S1;	**RELEASE** S2;

In case the tasks T1 and T2 are at the same time in their first critical region,
a deadlock results, because T1 is suspended by " **REQUEST** S2; " . (T2 has
already requested S2.) On the other hand T2 is suspended by " **REQUEST** S1; ".
If   in this case no release statement can be executed by another task the
suspensions remain constantly.

51

In order to avoid such situations lists of sema-variables can be used:

By executing the statement

REQUEST identifier§sema , ¨ ;

the executing task is suspended in case one of the corresponding sema
variables has the state "requested". This mentioned task is only allowed
to continue, if none of the sema variables has the state "requested"
anymore.
In case none of these sema variables has the state "requested" the executing task is continued - after decreasing the values of all sema variables
by 1.

The statement

RELEASE identifier§sema , ¨ ;

effects in the same way as if release statements would be executed without
interruption for all listed sema variables.
The deadlock of last mentioned example might have been avoided by
using the following program organization:

Task 1	Task 2
REQUEST S1, S2;	REQUEST S1, S2;
1. region	1. region
2. region	2. region
RELEASE S1, S2;	RELEASE S1, S2;

The sema variables may be listed in any order. (Of course, if no other
task would use S1 or S2, this example would also be programmed by
using only one sema variable.)

The general rules for declaration of sema variables as well as for request
and release statements are:

sema-declaration ::=
    (DECLARE / DCL)
    one-identifier-or-list (/ bound-list /) SEMA
    (/ resident-attribute /) (/ global-attribute /)
    (/ PRESET (simple-integer-constant-denotation , ¨) /) ;

request-statement ::=
   REQUEST name§sema , " ;

release-statement ::=
   RELEASE name§sema , " ;

The possibility of arrays of sema-variables exists also. The various elements of an array are used in the request- and release-statements by stating the identifier of the array followed by the index of the element.

Sema variables have to be declared at module level. At their declaration they can explicitly be initialized by

   PRESET (simple-integer-constant-denotation , ")

The constant denotations are assigned to the sema variables of the one-identifier-or-list in the sequence of their position.

Example:

   At their declaration the sema variables S1 and S2 should be given the values 3 and 5.

   DCL (S1, S2) **SEMA PRESET** (3, 5) ;

The global and resident attributes are explained in part III, paragraph 6 and 9.

4.4.2 Synchronization by means of Bolt Variables

Often the same data are used by different tasks and additional to this another task has to update these data.
In this case it should be guaranteed that the program parts for modification and for usage of data should be mutually exclusive; on the other hand simultaneous usage of data (by several tasks) is desired.

Principly these problems can be solved by the request and release statements, already described. However, this formulation is relatively complex and the duration of its execution is considerable. Out of this reason four additional statements are offered referring to so-called bolt variables.

A bolt variable can have the states "reserved", "free" or "entered", depending on the fact whether the attached resource is used exclusively, if it is available or if it is simultaneously used.

Bolt variables are declared as follows:

DCL one-identifier-or-list BOLT ;

After its declaration, a bolt variable has the state "free".

Let the bolt variable B be attached to some resource.
When entering a critical region concerning exclusive usage of this resource the access of other tasks is blocked by the statement

RESERVE B ;

When leaving this critical region the release results by the statement

FREE B ;

The critical regions concerning simultaneous usage of the resource are introduced and ended by the statements

ENTER B ; and LEAVE B ;

The more exact description concerning the effect of these statements considers the state and the modification of bolt variables:

Effect of RESERVE B ;

If B has the state "free" then B receives the state "reserved", other-wise the executing task will be suspended and will be enqueued into a queue attached to B.

Effect of FREE B ;

B is put in the state "free". Furthermore all tasks of the queue of B are dequeued. They in turn repeat their statements for reserve in the sequence of their priority.

Effect of ENTER B ;

If B has the state "reserved" or if a task is in the queue of B (based on a reserve statement), possessing the same or a higher priority then the executing task is suspended and enqueued into the queue of B. Otherwise B is put in the state "entered" to forbid exclusive access.

Also the (internally stated) number Z of entered (sharing) tasks is increased by one.

Effect of **LEAVE** B ;

If Z = 1, this statement equals to " **FREE** B ; ". Otherwise Z is decreased by 1 and B keeps the state "entered".

Example:

A Task MEASURING is taking values from a technical process, which are necessary for calculations made by the tasks MONITOR and DISPOSITION.
It should be guaranteed, however, that MEASURING only modifies the values, if they are not used. MONITOR and DISPOSITION should simultaneously use these values.

For this purpose one bolt variable VALUE is declared. The critical regions of modification or use of the values within the bodies of these 3 tasks are enclosed as follows:

In the body of MEASURING :

  . . .
RESERVE VALUE ;
modification
FREE VALUE ;
  . . .

In the bodies of MONITOR and DISPOSITION :

  . . .
ENTER VALUE ;
use
LEAVE VALUE ;
  . . .

All statements for bolt variables are also defined for lists of bolt variables, in analogy to the statements for sema variables.
Generally bolt variables may be declared and used as follows:

bolt-declaration ::=
    (**DECLARE** / **DCL**)
    one-identifier-or-list (/ bound-list /) **BOLT**
    (/ resident-attribute /) (/ global-attribute /) ;

```
bolt-statement ::=
    RESERVE  name§bolt , ¨ ;   /
    FREE     name§bolt , ¨ ;   /
    ENTER    name§bolt , ¨ ;   /
    LEAVE    name§bolt , ¨ ;
```

As the syntax shows it is also possible to declare arrays of bolt variables.
Bolt declarations have to be made at module level.

5. EXPRESSIONS , ASSIGNMENTS

5.1 Expressions

In previous paragraphs the notion expression was used without explanation
in some language features as for example:

- Use of an array element

   identifier (expression , ")

   e.g. TABLE (K, 2*I)

- Return statement

   RETURN (expression) ;

   e.g. **RETURN** (NO) ;

- Call of procedures

   list-of-actual-parameters ::= (expression , ")

   e.g. **CALL** P (A, TABLE (K, 2*I));

- Schedules for tasks

   AT expression§time

   e.g. **AT** 12:00:00 **ACTIVATE** T;

These examples show, that an expression might at least be

- a constant-denotation
- an identifier
- an identifier with index
- an arithmetic expression (e.g. 2*I).

Identifier and identifier with index are also known by the notion "name"
(see however III/1, Structures):

   name ::=

   identifier (/ (index , ") /)

   index ::=

   expression§which-yields-an-integer

The names stated within expressions must generally be names of scalar variables. However, it is permitted that also identifiers of arrays and structures are stated in the lists of output-statements (see 7.4, 7.5, 7.6).

Generally an expression has the form

    expression ::=
        (/ monadic-operator /) operand dyadic-operator **

Monadic operators have only one operand, dyadic operators have two operands.

    monadic-operator ::=
        + / - / NOT / new-monadic-operator

    dyadic-operator ::=
        + / - / * / $\underline{/}$ / $\underline{//}$ / ** / < / LT / > / GT /< = / LE / >= / GE /
        == / EQ / $\underline{/=}$ / NE / AND / OR / EXOR /></ CAT /< >/ CSHIFT /
        SHIFT / new-dyadic-operator

    operand ::=
        constant-denotation / name / function-call / conditional-expression /
        dereferencing / string-selection / (expression) / (assignment)

Examples:

-   -A + B * C - D / E ** 2
-   F (TABLE (K, 2*I)) / (F (I) - 3)
-   (A := B + C) / D
  results in A := B + C ; and A / B
-   A < B OR A < C
-   NEWIMAGE AND NOT OLDIMAGE
  the result is a bitstring with 1 in every position where OLDIMAGE
  has 0 and NEWIMAGE has 1.
-   XCOORD >< YCOORD >< ZCOORD
  results in a concatenation of these three bitstrings to one bitstring.

New-monadic-operator, new-dyadic-operator, dereferencing and string-selection are described in part III (paragraph 11, 4 and 2).

Conditional-expressions may occur in assignments and function procedures.

> conditional-expression ::=
>> IF expression§which-yields-B1
>>> THEN expression ELSE expression FIN

If the evaluation of the expression after IF yields '1'B (true), then the conditional-expression is replaced by the expression after THEN, otherwise it is replaced by the expression after ELSE .

Examples:

> (1) The function procedure MAX should determine the larger of two reals and return it.

>> MAX : PROC ((X, Y) FLOAT) RETURNS (FLOAT);
>>   RETURN (IF X >Y THEN X ELSE Y FIN);
>>   END ;
>>   . . .
>> A := MAX (B, C)/ 2;

> (2) Equivalent to this assignment is the following assignment:

>> A := (IF B >C THEN B ELSE C FIN)/ 2;

In order to influence the sequence of evaluation of an expression (see 5.1.3), parts of this expression can be set in parenthesis, e.g.

> A - (B + C)

5.1.1 Monadic Operators

The following table determines for every stated operator the possible type of its operand, the type of the result of the operation and the semantics of the operator.

In this table a stands for any operator, p for the precision of the operand and lg for its length.

syntax	type of operand a	type of result	semantics
+ a	FIXED (p) FLOAT (p) DURATION	FIXED (p) FLOAT (p) DURATION	---
- a	FIXED (p) FLOAT (p) DURATION	FIXED (p) FLOAT (p) DURATION	Inversion of the sign of a
NOT a	BIT (lg)	BIT (lg)	Inversion of all bits of a

Example:

```
DCL ( X, Y ) FLOAT, B BIT (4) ;
X := 3 ;
B := '1001'B ;
Y := -X ;  /* Y gets the value -3 */
B := NOT B ;  /* B gets the value '0110'B */
```

Further monadic operators, especially type conversion operators, are described in part III, paragraph 11.

5.1.2 Dyadic Operators

The following table determines for every stated operator the possible types of its operands, the type of the result of the operation and the semantics of the operator.

In this table a and b represent the first and the second operand, p1, p2, ... and lg1, lg2, ... stand for the precisions and lengths of operands and result.

Examples for the stated dyadic operators are described together with assignments (see 5.2).

Part II, paragraph 11, defines further dyadic operators.

60

syntax	type of a	type of b	type of result	semantics
a + b	FIXED(p1)	FIXED(p2)	FIXED(p3)	Addition of the values of
	FIXED(p1)	FLOAT(p2)	FLOAT(p3)	a and b.
	FLOAT(p1)	FIXED(p2)	FLOAT(p3)	p3 = max (p1, p2)
	FLOAT(p1)	FLOAT(p2)	FLOAT(p3)	
	DURATION	DURATION	DURATION	
	DURATION	CLOCK	CLOCK	
	CLOCK	DURATION	CLOCK	
a - b	FIXED(p1)	FIXED(p2)	FIXED(p3)	Subtraction of the values
	FIXED(p1)	FLOAT(p2)	FLOAT(p3)	of a and b.
	FLOAT(p1)	FIXED(p2)	FLOAT(p3)	p3 = max (p1, p2)
	FLOAT(p1)	FLOAT(p2)	FLOAT(P3)	
	DURATION	DURATION	DURATION	
	CLOCK	DURATION	CLOCK	
	CLOCK	CLOCK	DURATION	
a * b	FIXED(p1)	FIXED(p2)	FIXED(p3)	Multiplication of the
	FIXED(p1)	FLOAT(p2)	FLOAT(p3)	values of a and b.
	FLOAT(p1)	FIXED(p2)	FLOAT(p3)	p3 = max (p1, p2)
	FLOAT(p1)	FLOAT(p2)	FLOAT(p3)	
	FIXED(p1)	DURATION	DURATION	
	DURATION	FIXED(p2)	DURATION	
a / b	FIXED(p1)	FIXED(p2)	FLOAT(p3)	Division of the values
	FLOAT(p1)	FIXED(p2)	FLOAT(p3)	of a and b, if b $\neq$ 0.
	FIXED(p1)	FLOAT(p2)	FLOAT(p3)	
	FLOAT(p1)	FLOAT(p2)	FLOAT(p3)	
	DURATION	FIXED(p2)	DURATION	p3 = max (p1, p2)
a // b	FIXED(p1)	FIXED(p2)	FIXED(p3)	Integer division of the values of a and b, i.e. the result consists only of the integer part. p3 = max (p1, p2)

syntax	type of a	type of b	type of result	semantics
a ** b	FIXED(p1)	FIXED(p2)	FIXED(p1)	a*a*...*a (b times), if b > 0
				1 , if b = 0
	FLOAT(p1)	FIXED(p2)	FLOAT(p1)	a*a*...*a (b times), if b > 0
				1.0 , if b = 0
				1/(a*...*a) (lbl times), if b < 0
$a\left\{\begin{matrix}<\\LT\end{matrix}\right\}b$	FIXED(p1)	FIXED(p2)		Comparison "less than":
	FIXED(p1)	FLOAT(p2)		If the value of a is less than
	FLOAT(p1)	FIXED(p2)	BIT(1)	the value of b, then the result
	FLOAT(p1)	FLOAT(p2)		is '1'B else '0'B.
	CLOCK	CLOCK		
	DURATION	DURATION		
$a\left\{\begin{matrix}>\\GT\end{matrix}\right\}b$	see	see	BIT(1)	Comparison "greater than":
	a < b	a < b		If the value of a is greater than
				the value of b, then the result
				is '1'B else '0'B.
$a\left\{\begin{matrix}<=\\LE\end{matrix}\right\}b$	see	see	BIT(1)	Comparison "less or equal":
	a < b	a < b		If the value of a is less than or
				equal to the value of b, then
				the result is '1'B else '0'B.
$a\left\{\begin{matrix}>=\\GE\end{matrix}\right\}b$	see	see	BIT(1)	Comparison "greater or equal":
	a < b	a < b		If the value of a is greater than
				or equal to the value of b, then
				the result is '1'B else '0'B.
$a\left\{\begin{matrix}==\\EQ\end{matrix}\right\}b$	FIXED(p1)	FIXED(p2)		Comparison "equal to":
	FIXED(p1)	FLOAT(p2)		If the value of a is equal to the
	FLOAT(p1)	FIXED(p2)	BIT(1)	value of b, then the result is
	FLOAT(p1)	FLOAT(p2)		'1'B else '0'B.
	CLOCK	CLOCK		If lg2 ≠ lg1, then the shorter ope-
	DURATION	DURATION		rand is adjusted by adding |lg2 - lg1|
	CHAR(lg1)	CHAR(lg2)		blanks or '0'B resp. on the right.
	BIT(lg1)	BIT(lg2)		

syntax	type of a	type of b	type of result	semantics
$a\left\{\begin{matrix}/=\\NE\end{matrix}\right\}b$	FIXED(p1) FIXED(p1) FLOAT(p1) FLOAT(p1) CLOCK DURATION CHAR(lg1) BIT(lg1)	FIXED(p2) FLOAT(p2) FIXED(p2) FLOAT(p2) CLOCK DURATION CHAR(lg2) BIT(lg2)	BIT(1)	Comparison "not equal to": If the value of a is not equal to the value of b, then the result is '1'B else '0'B.
a AND b	BIT(lg1)	BIT(lg2)	BIT(lg3)	$lg3 = \max(lg1, lg2)$ The length of the shorter ope- rand is adjusted by adding
a OR b	BIT(lg1)	BIT(lg2)	BIT(lg3)	$\|lg1 - lg2\|$ '0'B on the right. The corresponding single bits are logically connected according
a EXOR b	BIT(lg1)	BIT(lg2)	BIT(lg3)	to the following table (0, 1 stand short for '0'B and '1'B, resp.):

a	b	a AND b	a OR b	a EXOR b
1	1	1	1	0
1	0	0	1	1
0	1	0	1	1
0	0	0	0	0

syntax	type of a	type of b	type of result	semantics
$a\left\{\begin{matrix}><\\CAT\end{matrix}\right\}b$	CHAR(lg1) BIT(lg1)	CHAR(lg2) BIT(lg2)	CHAR(lg3) BIT(lg3)	Concatenation: The result is a character- or bitstring of length $lg3 = lg1+lg2$, which consists of string a, followed by string b.
$a\left\{\begin{matrix}<>\\CSHIFT\end{matrix}\right\}b$	BIT(lg)	FIXED(p)	BIT(lg)	Cyclic shift of a b bits to the left, if b > 0 $\|b\|$ bits to the right, if b < 0.
a SHIFT b	BIT(lg)	FIXED(p)	BIT(lg)	a is shifted $\|b\|$ bits to the left, if b > 0, and to the right, if b < 0. Zeros are added from the right or left, resp.

5.1.3 Evaluation of Expressions

Let a, b, c, ... be constants or scalar variables.

According to the rules of arithmetics the evaluation of an expression depends on the precedence of its operators. E.g., the dyadic operator "*" has a higher precedence than the dyadic operator "+" : evaluating the expression "a+b*c" first "b*c" is calculated and then the result is added to a.

The following list defines the precedence for dyadic operators; lower numbers indicate higher precedence.

precedence	dyadic operators
1	**
2	*, /, ><, //
3	+, -, <>, SHIFT
4	< , > ,<=,>=
5	==, /=
6	AND
7	OR, EXOR

The monadic operators +, - and NOT have the precedence 1.

In addition the sequence of evaluation of an expression is influenced as usual by enclosing parts of the expression in parenthesis. Evaluating the expression

$$a * (b - (c - d))$$

first c - d is calculated, this first intermediate result is subtracted from b and then this second intermediate result is multiplied by a.

Generally the evaluation of an expression follows the rules listed below:

- First that part of an expression is evaluated, which contains the operator with the highest precedence. This only applies, if one of the following rules isn't violated.

- If subsequent operators have the same precedence, then the expression is evaluated

- from left to right, if $2 \leqslant$ precedence $\leqslant 7$

   Example: $a - b + c$ is equivalent to $(a - b) + c$

- from right to left, if precedence $= 1$

   Example: $-a ** b$ is equivalent to $- (a ** b)$

   $a**b**b$ is equivalent to $a**(b**c)$

- Parts of the expression which are enclosed in parenthesis are evaluated completely following the above rules before they are combined with other parts of the expression.

Example:

$$(a * (b - c)) ** d < e + f (x) \quad \text{AND} \quad h / (i + j) >= (k - l) * m$$

The braces show, which parts of this expression are built and are combined with other parts when evaluating the whole expression.

5.2 Assignments

Assignments are only defined concerning scalar variables and structures (see III/1).

   assignment ::=
      name $(:= / =)^{**}$ expression ;

This statement results to the fact, that the value of the mentioned expression is assigned to all variables stated left to the assignment symbol $:=$ or $=$. During execution of this statement the value of the expression is evaluated; afterwards one can refer to this value by means of the names of the variables:

   RESULT (I) := KOEFF * SIN ((X (I+1) - X (I)) / X (I));

The type of variables positioned left to the assignment symbol and the type of the value of the expression must be identical, however, with the following exceptions:

- The value of a FIXED variable and/or an integer may be assigned to a FLOAT variable.

65

- The precision of a variable left to the assignment symbol can be larger than the precision of the value of the expression.

- The length of a bit string and/or character string stated left to the assignment symbol may be larger than the value to be assigned; in this case this value is adjusted by adding zeros or blanks on the right.

Operators concerning necessary type conversions are described in III/11.

Examples:

```
DCL ( I, J ) FIXED (12) , K  FIXED (31),
    ( X, Y ) FLOAT,
    BIT 8 BIT (8),  BIT12  BIT (12),
    TEXT4 CHAR (4),  TEXT10 CHAR (10),
    DURATIONS (2) DURATION,
    TIME (2) CLOCK;

I := 2.0;               /* WRONG */
J := K := 3;
X := J + 5;  Y := 0;
K := J;
J := K;                 /* WRONG */
TEXT10 := 'RESULT';     /* TEXT10 HAS THE VALUE 'RESULT⌴⌴' */
BIT8 := 'A9F'B4;        /* WRONG, BECAUSE TOO LONG */
DURATIONS(1) := 1 HRS;
DURATIONS(2) := 30 MIN;
TIME(1) := 11:00:00;
TIME(2) := TIME(1) + ( IF  TIME(1) < 12:00:00  THEN  DURATIONS(1)
                                        ELSE DURATIONS(2)  FIN );

BIT8 := '10001100'B;
BIT12 := BIT8 >< '11';   /* BIT12 HAS THE VALUE '100011001100'B */
BIT8 := BIT8 CSHIFT 3;   /* BIT8 HAS THE VALUE '01100100'B */
BIT12 := BIT12 SHIFT -6; /* BIT12 HAS THE VALUE '000000100011'B */
```

The possibility of associating variables with an invariant attribute for protecting them from assignments is given (see III/8).

6.   SEQUENCE CONTROL STATEMENTS

The declaration of a task or procedure defines a series of statements
which at runtime are executed in the given order unless this order is
altered by the appropriate control statements.
These are the following:

- goto statement
- if statement
- case statement
- dummy statement
- loop statement

6.1   Goto Statement

goto-statement ::=
    GOTO identifier§label ;

This statement has the effect that the program execution continues
at that point in the program indicated by the label. This point must be
a statement within the task body containing the goto statement.

Example:

MEASUREMENT: READING: READ VALUE FROM DEVICE ;
    . . .
    GOTO READING;

A statement may, in general, be associated with one or more labels
(identifiers), i.e. the labels are placed immediately preceding the statement and separated from it and from each other by means of colons.

6.2   If Statement

The if statement is used to determine, according to the result of an
expression, at which point in the program the execution shall continue.

> if-statement ::=
>> IF expression **THEN** statement ··· (/ **ELSE** statement ··· /) **FIN;**

The result of the expression must be of type BIT(1). If the expression
yields the value '1'B (true) then the statements following **THEN** are
executed, otherwise the statements following **ELSE** (if any).
Provided the execution of the statements following **THEN** or **ELSE**
has not resulted in a jump out of the if-statement the statements following
FIN are then executed.

Example:

```
IF  GRADIENT > GRADLIMIT
     THEN GOTO  ALARM ;
     ELSE IF  GRADIENT > GRADTHRESHOLD
             THEN ALL 1 SEC ACTIVATE READING ;
                  /* CHECK MORE FREQUENTLY */
         FIN ;
FIN ;
output to log

. . .
```

The log is output when GRADIENT is less or equal GRADLIMIT.

68

6.3   Case Statement and Dummy Statement

Suppose a (function) procedure MONITOR is to be used to control several
similar devices, returning after each call a number between 1 and 4 with
the following significance:

-    return value = 1 : execution successful
-    return value = 2: arguments invalid
-    return value = 3: device not answering
-    return value = 4: device malfunction

The task SUPPLY is then to take appropriate action.

The case statement is provided for programming such decisions.

```
case-statement ::=
    CASE expression
        ( ALT statement ··· ) ···
        (/ OUT statement ··· /)
    FIN ;
```

The statements following the first ALT (alternative 1) correspond to
the value 1, those following the second ALT (alternative 2) to the value 2
and so on.

When executing a case statement the given expression is first evaluated.
It must yield a value of type FIXED. If the value lies between 1 and
the number of given alternatives then the corresponding statements
are executed, otherwise those statements following OUT (if any).
Provided the execution of the selected statements has not resulted in
a jump out of the case statement those statements following FIN are
next executed.

Example:

The above problem might be programmed as follows:

SUPPLY: **TASK PRIO** 7 ;

MONITOR : **PROC** (NO **FIXED** /* DEVICE */ ,
JOB **BIT**(8) /* JOB DATA */)
RETURNS (**FIXED**);
procedure body to deal with job
END ; /* MONITOR */
. . .
creation of JOB for device no. NO

AGAIN : **CASE** MONITOR (NO, JOB)
ALT /* EXECUTION SUCCESSFUL */
;
ALT /* ARGUMENTS INVALID */
CALL ERROR (2) ; **GOTO** FINISH ;
ALT /* DEVICE NOT ANSWERING */
ACTIVATE DEVICEBREAKDOWN **PRIO** 2 ;
CALL ERROR (3) ; **GOTO** FINISH ;
ALT /* DEVICE MALFUNCTION */
CALL DEVICECONTROL ; **GOTO** AGAIN ;
OUT /* RESULT OUT OF RANGE */
CALL ERROR (5) ;
FIN ;
. . .
FINISH : **END** ; /* SUPPLY */

The dummy-statement " ; " is used in this example. It has no effect
and is only of interest in if statements and case statements. In this
example the " ; " causes the statements following **FIN** to be executed
in the successful case ("execution successful").
The dummy statement has the form:

dummy-statement ::=
;

70

6.4 Loop Statement

It is frequently necessary to repeat a series of statements changing only one parameter. For example suppose that several devices are to be tested (let NUMBER be the number of devices):

```
FOR I FROM 1 BY 1 TO NUMBER
        REPEAT
            testing of DEVICE (I)
        END ;
```

Such program loops have in general the following form:

```
loop-statement ::=
        (/ FOR identifier§loop-variable /)
        (/ FROM expression§start /)
        (/ BY expression§step /)
        (/ TO expression§end /)
        (/ WHILE expression§condition /)
        REPEAT
            (/ declaration ··· /) (/ statement ··· /)
        END ;
```

Those declarations and statements which follow REPEAT, the loop body, are carried out as many times as determined by the preceding loop control, thereafter those statements following END. It is however possible to leave the loop by means of a goto statement. It is not possible to jump into a loop body.

Any statements are permitted within a loop; in particular loops may be nested:

```
FOR I TO 10
    REPEAT
        FOR K TO 10
            REPEAT
                C (I, K) := A (I, K) + B (I, K) ;
            END ;
    END ;
```

71

Where start or step values are omitted the value 1 is assumed. Where the end value is omitted the loop body may be repeated without limit.

The loop variable may neither be declared nor changed. It has the implicit type **FIXED**. The values of the expressions given for start, step and end must be of type **FIXED**, the value of the expression given for the condition must be of type **BIT** (1). The loop variable may not be used in these expressions, except in the condition expression, but may be used in the loop body.

In addition all rules for blocks apply equally to loop bodies (see III/5).

The following flow diagram is an equivalent representation of the statement:

    FOR identifier§loop-variable
    FROM expression§start
    BY expression§step
    TO expression§end
    WHILE expression§condition
    REPEAT
        loop-body
    END ;

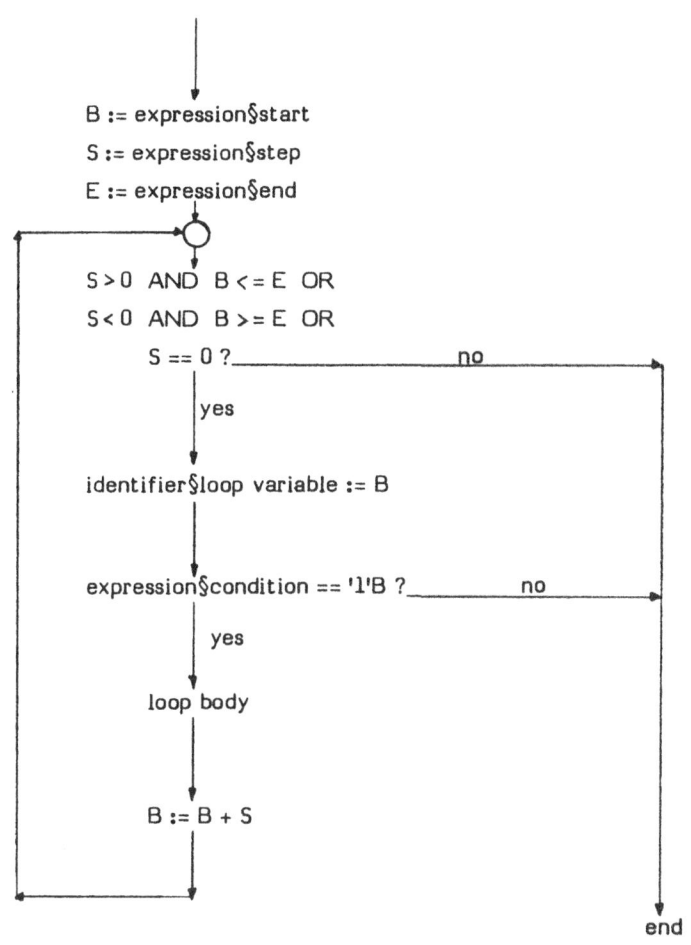

B := expression§start
S := expression§step
E := expression§end

S > 0 AND B < = E OR
S < 0 AND B > = E OR
    S == 0 ?_____no

        yes

identifier§loop variable := B

expression§condition == '1'B ?_____no

        yes

    loop body

    B := B + S

                                        end

7.   INPUT , OUTPUT

The input and output statements of PEARL allow to transfer data from
the working storage to an external data station (output) and vice versa
(input). Generally data stations are standard peripheral devices (printer,
card reader, TTY, disk, magnetic tape etc) or process control devices
(measuring devices, regulators, interrupting devices etc).

In addition the PEARL programmer can create user defined data stations
upon these system defined data stations in order to exchange data with
files on disks, magnetic tapes, printers etc.

The data stations are referred to in the I/O-statements by freely choosable,
logical user names. Traditional programming languages usually attach
logical names of data stations to devices of a special configuration by
means of an extra computer dependent job control language. In PEARL
these attachments are made within the program in a uniform manner:
all system defined data stations to be used in the program have to be
declared in the system division by listing their (computer dependent)
system names and by attaching freely chosen user-names to them.
In order to use these system defined data stations in I/O statements
of the problem division they have to be specified there with their user
names (see 7.2). User defined data stations are declared only in the
problem division.

7.1   System Division

The system division is to describe the configuration needed for the in-
put/output of the program. This description must contain at least the
system and user names of the system defined data stations which are
to be used in the program. For test and documentation purposes it may
contain in addition the description of the connections of these system
defined data stations.

The devices, signals and interrupts of a specific computer system have specific system names. We shall use the following arbitrary system names in the examples of this chapter:

System name	Device
CPU	central processor unit
INT	interrupt device
ANIN	analog input device
DIGIN	digital input device
ANOUT	analog output device
MULXCH	multiplex channel
SELCH	selective channel
DISP	display

When using several devices of the same type they may be distinguished by an index following their name, i.e. a system name generally has the form

system-name ::=
    identifier (/ (integer-constant-denotation) /)

For example, 5 displays may have the system-names DISP(1), DISP(2), ..., DISP(5).

For most of the devices of the technical process it is necessary to describe their connection points with the digital or analog or interrupt device of the computer system. Connection points are described by digits or identifiers following the system name of the device. E.g. an analog input device may have 32 connection points for analog input, one connection with the interrupt device and one connection with a multiplex channel. The connection points for analog input may be attached with the numbers 1 to 32, the connection points for the connections with the interrupt device and the multiplex channel may be identified with I and M (see the following picture).

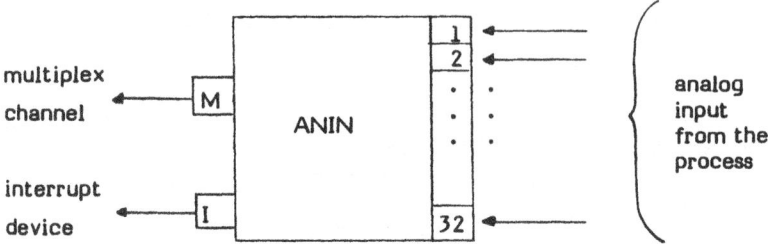

A connection point is described as follows:

    connection-point ::=
        system-name * (identifier / integer-constant-denotation)

Therefore the 34 connection-points of ANIN may have the system-names

    ANIN*1 , ANIN*2 , . . . , ANIN*32 , ANIN*I and ANIN*M .

Connections of devices of the computer system are described by means
of arrows denoting the flow of information:

    connection ::=
        connection-point (< - / -> / <->) connection-point ;

The next example is related to the following picture of a specific configuration:

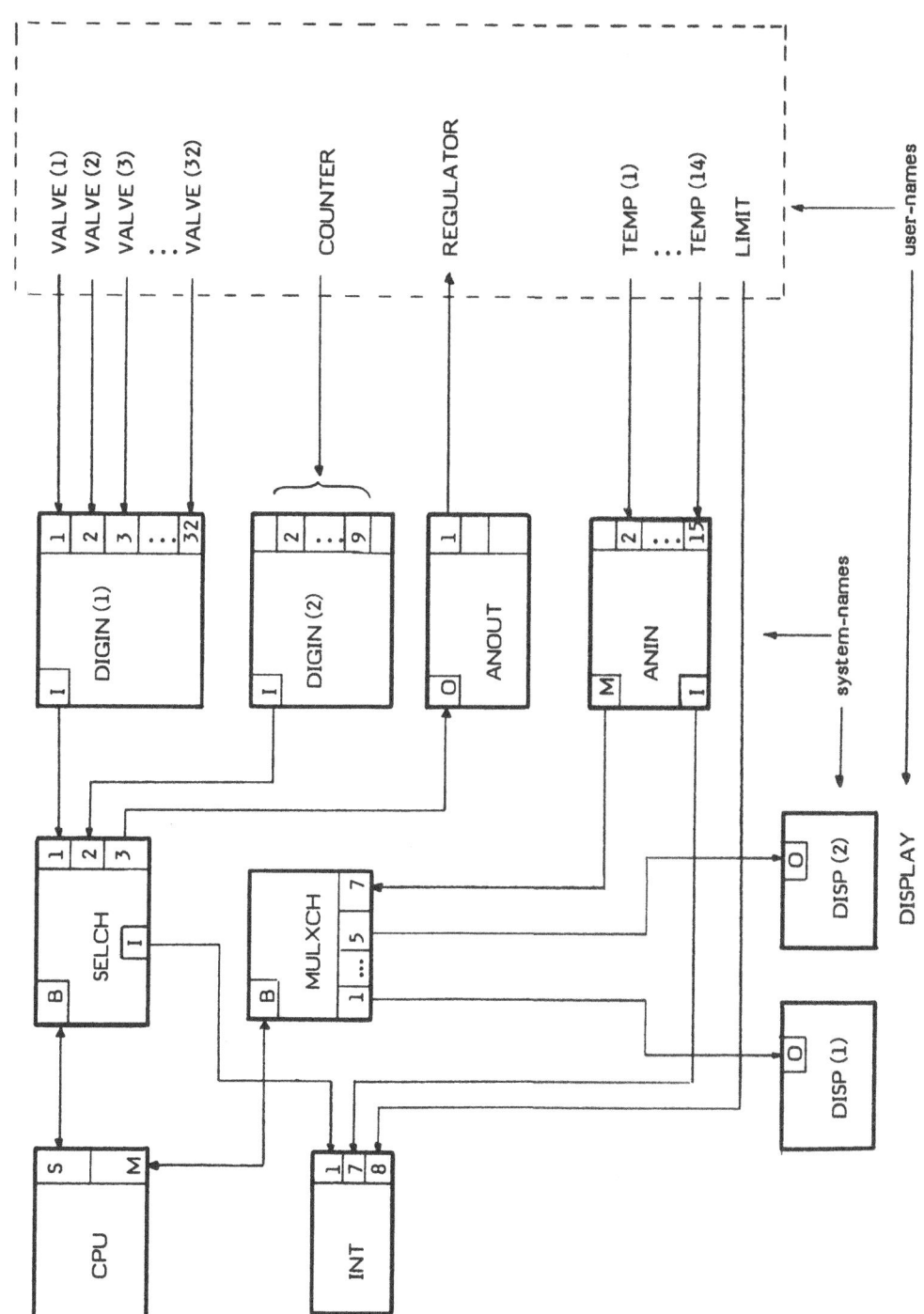

```
MODULE ( EXAMPLE ) ;
SYSTEM ;

/* CONNECTIONS OF DEVICES OF THE COMPUTER SYSTEM */

CPU * S <-> SELCH * B ;
            SELCH * 1 < - DIGIN (1) * I ;
            SELCH * 2 <- DIGIN (2) * I ;
            SELCH * 3 -> ANOUT * O ;
CPU * M <-> MULXCH * B ;
            MULXCH * 1  -> DISP (1) * O ;
            MULXCH * 2  -> DISP (2) * O ;
            MULXCH * 7 <-  ANIN * M ;
INT * 1 <- SELCH * I ;
INT * 7 <- ANIN * I ;

/* ATTACHING USER NAMES TO SYSTEM NAMES */

VALVE (1:32) :   DIGIN (1) * (1:32) ;
COUNTER :        DIGIN (2) * 2, 8 ;      /* 8 CONNECTION POINTS */
REGULATOR :      ANOUT * 1 ;
TEMP (1:14) :    ANIN * (2:15) ;
LIMIT :          INT * 8 ;
DISPLAY :        DISP (2) ;
 . . .
```

Generally, system defined data stations, interrupts and signals have to be declared as follows in the system division:

```
declaration-of-system-defined-data-station  ::=
    identifier§user-name  (/ ( index-bounds ) /) : system-name
        (/  * ( identifier / int / ( index-bounds )) (/ , int§width /) /)
        (/ < - / -> / < - > /) ;

index-bounds  ::=
    int : int
```

int ::=

   integer-constant-denotation

This declaration attaches also the user name of a data station to its
system name.

All possible system defined data stations of a certain PEARL implementation are listed together with their system names in the corresponding
user manual (implementation handbook).

Further possibilities for complex configurations are described in III/14.

7.2   Definition of Data Stations in the Problem Division

System defined data stations, which are declared in the system division
of a PEARL program, must be specified with their user names in any
problem division where they are to be used.

Example:

    MODULE (EXAMPLE);
    SYSTEM ;
    VALVE (1:32) :   DIGIN (1) * (1:32) ;
    DISPLAY :   DISP (2) ;
    . . .

    PROBLEM ;
    SPC VALVE ( ) DATION IN BASIC ,
        DISPLAY DATION OUT ALPHIC ... ;
    . . .

Arrays of data stations are specified with a virtual bound list like arrays
in the list of formal parameters of a procedure.

79

Generally data stations are specified as follows:

dation-specification ::=
    (SPECIFY / SPC)
    one-identifier-or-list (/ ( ) /) dation-mode
    (/ resident-attribute /) (/ global-attribute /) ;

dation-mode ::=
    DATION sink-source-attribute class
    (/ topology access /) (/ control attribute /)

The different attributes allow to check at compile time the compatibility
between the properties of system defined data stations and their use
in the program.

User defined data stations have to be declared in the problem division:

dation-declaration ::=
    (DECLARE / DCL)
    one-identifier-or-list (/ bound-list /) dation-mode
    (/ resident-attribute /) (/ global-attribute /)
    CREATED (name§system-defined-data-station) ;

One dimensional arrays of dations may be declared.

In specifying or declaring a data station it must be stated, whether this
data station is source and/or sink of data transfers.

sink-source-attribute ::=
    IN / OUT / INOUT

A data station defined with IN is source of data, i.e. it may be used
only in input statements (transferring data from this data station
into the working storage). Examples are digital input devices and card
reader.
Data stations defined with OUT may be used only as sinks of data in
output statement, e.g. for printers.

Data stations defined with **INOUT** may be used in input and output statements, e.g. for disks.

PEARL offers three kinds of input/output statements:

. Read/write statements for the transfer of data (transfer items) with computer internal representation. Typical examples are transfers to disks or magnetic tapes.

. Get/put statements for "formatted" input/output, i.e. for the transfer of transfer items with transformation between the computer internal representation and the representation possible on the data station in question. Typical examples are transfers to printers or displays.

. Take/send statements for process I/O.

A data station allows only one kind of data transfer which is stated by the class attribute:

class ::=
      ALPHIC / **BASIC** / transfer-item-type

transfer-item-type ::=
      ALL / simple-mode / compound-mode

simple-mode ::=
      type-integer / type-real / type-bit-string /
      type-character-string / type-clock / type-duration

ALPHIC denotes that the data station is able to represent its data (transfer items) in alpha-numerical form; data transfers to or from this data station must be made by put/get statements.

A data station with the attribute **BASIC** is a data station in the technical process to be controlled; data transfers to or from this data station have to be made by send/take statements.

81

A data station with the attribute transfer-item-type is able to store data of the specified type in computer internal representation; data transfers to or from this data station have to be made by write/read statements.

Compound-mode will be explained in part III, paragraph 14. The attribute **ALL** implies all possibilities of simple-mode or compound-mode.

Example:

Two files (**INPUT** and **RESULTS**) are to be created on a disk having the system name D25 and the user name DISK. INPUT shall have data of type **FIXED** (15) in computer internal format which are to be read, and RESULTS shall be source and sink of data of type **FLOAT** (15) in computer internal format.

```
MODULE (EXAMPLE );
SYSTEM ;

DISK : D25 ;

PROBLEM ;
SPC DISK DATION INOUT ALL ... ;
DCL INPUT DATION IN FIXED (15) ... CREATED ( DISK ),
     RESULTS DATION INOUT FLOAT (15) ... CREATED ( DISK );
. . .
DCL NEXTINPUT FIXED (15),
     RESULT FLOAT (15);
. . .
READ NEXTINPUT FROM INPUT ;
. . .
WRITE RESULT TO RESULTS ;
. . .
```

All data stations have to be declared or specified with the source-sink-attribute and the class attribute. The attributes described now are optional.

Depending on their properties data-stations can store one or more transfer items, i.e. values of objects the type of them being specified by the
attribute transfer-item-type. If the properties of a data station allow
to do so, several transfer-items can build one line and several lines can
build one page. In doing so the set of data of the data station is arranged
as a 1- or 2- or 3-dimensional array. With other words, a data station can
have a certain topology, which is described by the corresponding attribute in its declaration and/or specification:

> topology ::=
>   DIM ((/ * / int /) (/ , (/ int /) (/ , (/ int /) /) /)) (/ TFU (/ MAX /) /)

In a specification the integer constant denotations or the asterisk resp.
must be omitted; they must not be omitted in a declaration.

The integer constant denotations represent the values of the upper
bounds of the dimensions of the data station's topology (array). The
lower bounds are always 1. The rightmost denotation of int always
specifies the number of items per line, the next (optional) denotation
left from the rightmost one specifies the number of lines per page and
the third (optional) denotation specifies the number of pages. An asterisk
in the leftmost position means, that the number of corresponding elements
(items or lines or pages) is unlimited. A printer with 120 items (characters)
per line, 60 lines per page and arbitrary many pages would have the topology
DIM (*, 60, 120).

The following combinations are possible in declarations:

- 3-dimensional topology
  DIM (number of pages, number of lines, number of items)
  DIM (*, number of lines, number of items)

- 2-dimensional topology
  DIM (number of lines, number of items)
  DIM (*, number of items)

- 1-dimensional topology
  DIM (number of items)
  DIM (*)

83

The attribute topology also describes the transfer unit of a data station, i.e. how many items are transferred to or from this data station by execution of one I/O statement for this data station.

.   If **TFU** and **MAX** are omitted, the transfer unit is one transfer item.

.   If **TFU** or **TFU MAX** is supplied the transfer unit is one line of transfer items, i.e. the PEARL system implicitly supplies a buffer for one line.
    If the actual number of transfer items in an input/output statement is less than the number of items in one line, then the line in question is filled up implicitly with blanks in the case of an **ALPHIC** data station; in other cases it is filled up with zeros.

Example:

        . . .
        DCL PRINTER **DATION OUT ALPHIC DIM** (*, 60, 120) **TFU** . . . ,
            RESULTS **DATION INOUT FLOAT** (15) **DIM** (100, 10) /* NO TFU */ . . . ;
        . . .
        PUT ' PEARL ' **TO** PRINTER ;
        WRITE 1.0 **TO** RESULTS ;
        . . .

    The put statement effects the output of the 5 characters P,
    E, A, R and L followed by 115 blanks in one (new) line of PRINTER.

    The write statement effects <u>logically</u> only the output of one value
    1.0 to RESULTS .

The access mode of a data station has to be described in the attribute

    access ::=
        DIRECT / FORWARD / FORBACK
        (/ NOCYCL /) / CYCLIC
        (/ STREAM /) / NOSTREAM

DIRECT means, that any transfer item within the array defined by the topology may be selected by denoting its <u>absolute</u> position in the array (see 7.4, 7.5).

FORWARD and **FORBACK** mean, that the transfer items of this data station can only be reached in sequential order, eventually with specifying the <u>relative</u> position of an item in relation to the item just accessed (see 7.4, 7.5). In the case of **FORWARD** this relative position has to lead to a higher index in the n-dimensional topology.

NOCYCL , **CYCLIC** , **STREAM** and **NOSTREAM** will be explained in context with the I/O statements in paragraph 7.4 and 7.5.

When explicit transformation or explicit positioning is intended in I/O statements for a certain data station, this data station has to be specified and/or declared with the control-attribute.

> control-attribute ::=
>> **CONTROL** (<u>ALL</u>)

7.3   Opening and Closing Data Stations

User defined data stations have to be opened before using them in I/O statements.

> open-statement ::=
>> **OPEN** name§dation (/ BY open-parameter , ˙ ˙ /) ;

After execution of an open statement for a data station with topology, the actual position is equal to the start position ((1, 1, 1) or (1, 1) or (1) resp.).

The open parameters allow to choose an identification and a disposition for the physical data set belonging to a data station. There exists e.g. a data set TABLE-1 on a disk. This data set can be attached to a user defined data station (say TABLE) by executing an open statement for this data station with the identification TABLE-1 as parameter:

> **OPEN** TABLE **BY** IDF (TABLE-1);

Generally the following parameters are possible:

open-parameter ::=
　　　(IDF ((name§character-string / character-string-constant-denotation))) /
　　　OLD / NEW / ANY / CAN / PRM

Semantics:

.　IDF

　　The value of the specified character variable or the specified character
　　string constant is the name of a data set which is to be identified
　　with the data station specified by name§dation in the open statement.

.　OLD

　　IDF must be stated. A data set with the IDF-name must exist.

.　NEW

　　IDF must be stated. A new data set with the IDF-name is to be created.
　　There must not already exist a data set having this IDF-name.

.　ANY

　　If a data set with the IDF-name exists, it is reopened; if not, a new
　　data set with the IDF-name is to be created. If IDF is omitted the
　　PEARL system creates a name for the data set.

.　CAN

　　The data set is to be cancelled after closing the data station, i.e.
　　it shall not be possible to reopen it.

.　PRM

　　The data set shall be permanent after closing the data station, i.e.
　　it shall be possible to reopen it by execution of an open statement
　　with the same IDF-name.

Default parameters are ANY and PRM.

By execution of a close statement the specified data station is closed, i.e. it can only be used again after execution of an open statement (see below for details).

```
close-statement ::=
    CLOSE name§dation (/ BY close-parameter , ˙ ˙ /) ;


close-parameter ::=
    CAN / PRM
```

General rules:

.   Several tasks may use a data station at the same time. It is not necessary that every task executes an open or close statement. However at least one open statement has to be executed before a user defined data station can be used.

.   A data station is closed, if as many close statements as open statements have been executed for this data station.

.   Corresponding open and close statements can be executed by different tasks.

.   Execution of an open or close statement with parameters CAN or PRM superscribes an earlier executed open or close statement concerning the effect of these parameters.

Example:

```
MODULE ( EXAMPLE );

SYSTEM ;
PRINTER : LP ;
DISK : DIRECTORY ;

PROBLEM ;
SPC PRINTER DATION OUT ALPHIC DIM ( *, 60, 120 )
    FORWARD CONTROL ( ALL );
SPC DISK DATION INOUT ALL CONTROL ( ALL );
DCL TABLE DATION INOUT FLOAT (15) DIM ( 300, 5 ) DIRECT
    CONTROL ( ALL ) CREATED ( DISK );
```

```
START : TASK ;
    OPEN TABLE BY IDF ('TAB-1'), OLD ;
    ACTIVATE PROT ;
    . . .
    END ;
PROT : TASK ;
    I/O statements with PRINTER and TABLE
    . . .
    CLOSE TABLE ;
    END ;
. . .
MODEND ;
```

7.4 Read and Write Statement

The read statement is to put in, the write statement is to put out data without transforming them (binary I/O). The data stations in question have to be defined with the attribute "transfer-item-type".

Examples:

(1) The columns 4 and 5 in the topology of the data station TABLE (see 7.4) have to be replaced by actual values.

```
. . .
DCL (X, Y, Z) FLOAT (15);
. . .
FOR LINE FROM 1 TO 300 REPEAT
    calculation of X, Y, Z
    WRITE X, SIN(Y + Z) TO TABLE BY POS (LINE, 4);
END ;
. . .
```

(2) A task LOGGING is measuring periodically 14 values of temperature; after processing the task writes them sequentially in blocks of 14 values into a logbook on a magnetic tape.

```
MODULE ( EXAMPLE );

SYSTEM ;
TEMP ( 1:14 ): ANIN * ( 2 : 15 );
TAPE : MT (3);

PROBLEM ;
SPC TEMP ( ) DATION IN BASIC ,
    TAPE DATION INOUT ALL ;
DCL LOGBOOK DATION OUT FIXED (15) DIM ( *, 14 ) TFU
    FORWARD CREATED ( TAPE );

START : TASK ;
    OPEN LOGBOOK ;
    ALL 10 SEC ACTIVATE LOGGING ;
    . . .
    END ;

LOGGING :  TASK ;
    DCL TEMPERATURE (14) FIXED (15) ;
    FOR I FROM 1 TO 14 REPEAT
        TAKE TEMPERATURE ( I ) FROM TEMP ( I );
    END ;
    processing ·
    WRITE TEMPERATURE TO LOGBOOK ;
    END ;
. . .
MODEND ;
```

The general syntax of the read and write statements is as follows:

```
read-statement ::=
    READ (/ ( name§variable / slice ) , ˙ ˙ /)
    FROM name§dation (/ BY position , ˙ ˙ /) ;


write-statement ::=
    WRITE (/ ( expression / slice ) , ˙ ˙ /)
    TO name§dation (/ BY position , ˙ ˙ /) ;


slice ::=
    identifier§array ( (/ - /) simple-integer-constant-denotation :
                       (/ - /) simple-integer-constant-denotation )


position ::=
    absolute-position / relative-position


absolute-position ::=
    COL ( expression )   /
    LINE ( expression )   /
    POS ( expression (/ , expression (/ , expression /) /) )


relative-expression ::=
    X (/ ( expression ) /)          /
    SKIP (/ ( expression ) /)       /
    PAGE (/ ( expression ) /)       /
    ADV ( expression (/ , expression (/ , expression /) /) )
```

When executing a read statement the transfer items determined by
position are read one after another and assigned to the corresponding
variables in the stated list of names and slices ("list of variables").
These assignments obey the general rules for assignments. If an object
of the list of variables is an array, then the determined transfer items
are assigned line by line; if it is a structure, then the transfer items
are assigned to the components of the structure in correspondence with
the sequence determined by the declaration of the structure (see III/ 1).

For easier writing subsequent elements of an array can be written as slice in the list of variables. Let LIST be an array with ten elements LIST (1) , . . . , LIST (10) ; then the following both statements are equivalent:

    READ LIST (2) , LIST (3) , LIST (4) FROM . . . ;
    READ LIST (2:4) FROM . . . ;

The list of positions is evaluated completely before the transfer items corresponding to the list of variables are read sequentially starting with the position evaluated last (i.e. stated rightmost in the list of positions).

Example:

    "Read X and Y from FILE by position 3 and position 5"
    is equivalent to

    READ X FROM FILE BY POS (3) ;
    READ Y FROM FILE BY POS (5) ;

    This is not equivalent to

    READ X , Y FROM FILE BY POS (3) , POS (5) ;

    Executing this statement X is read from position 5 and Y is read from the position subsequent to 5.

These rules apply analogously to the write statement.

The types of the listed scalar variables, the types of the elements of the listed arrays and structures and the types of the results of the listed expressions must be compatible with the transfer-item-type of the data station.

The list of variables or expressions may be omitted, if a read or write statement shall be used only for positioning. In this case a position must be supplied.

The elements in the list of position refer to the topology (array) of the data station; they determine the data items to be transferred. Therefore their values must be of type FIXED and compatible to the topology.

Absolute positioning i.e. positioning independently from the actual position is allowed only for data stations having the access attribute DIRECT. Relative positions state the distance from the actual position; in this case a data station must have the access attribute FORWARD, FORBACK or DIRECT.

In detail the semantics of the positions is as follows:

. COL (expression)

refers to the first dimension of the topology and determines item i in the actual line, if i is equal to the value of the expression. Equivalent: POS (expression)

. LINE (expression)

refers to the second dimension of the topology and determines line i in the actual page, if i is equal to the value of the expression. Equivalent: POS (expression , 1)

Example:

The topology (5, 10) represents a 2-dimensional array:

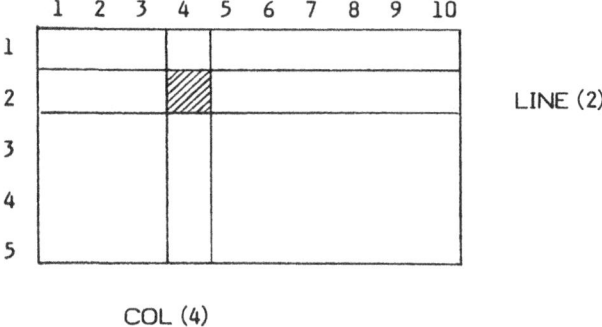

COL (4)

. POS $\underline{(}$ expression $(/,$ expression $(/,$ expression $/)$ $/)$ $\underline{)}$

refers to the position of an item in the n-dimensional topology
(n = 1, 2, 3) of a data station. Missing expressions are replaced by
the corresponding actual positions.

Example:

When executing the statement

READ X FROM FILE BY POS (3, 2, 8);

the 8th item of the second line of the third page of FILE is read.
If subsequently the statement

READ X FROM FILE BY POS (4, 5);

would be executed then the fifth element of line 4 of the same
page (no. 3) of FILE would be read.

Let i indicate the values of the expressions stated below.

. X $(/ \underline{(}$ expression $\underline{)}$ $/)$

refers to the first dimension of the topology and determines the
i-th item after (i positive) or before (i negative) the actual item
in the actual line of the data station; i = 0 determines the actual
item.

X is equivalent to X (1), X (expression) is equivalent to
ADV (expression) .

. SKIP $(/ \underline{(}$ expression $\underline{)}$ $/)$

refers to the second dimension of the topology and determines the
beginning (first item) of the i-th line after (i positive) or before
(i negative) the actual line of the actual page of the data station;
i = 0 determines the beginning of the actual line.

SKIP is equivalent to SKIP (1), SKIP (expression) is equivalent
to ADV (expression) 1 $\underline{)}$.

.   PAGE (/ (expression) /)

refers to the third dimension of the topology and determines the
beginning (first item of the first line) of the i-th line after (i positive) or before (i negative) the actual page of the data station;
i = 0 determines the beginning of the actual page.
PAGE is equivalent to PAGE (1) , PAGE (expression) is equivalent to ADV (expression , 1 , 1).

If the data station has the access attribute **FORWARD** then i must
be positive.

.   ADV (expression (/ , expression (/ , expression /) /))

determines the distance of the transfer item to the actual item.
Missing expressions are replaced by zero. The value of the leftmost
expression must be positive if the data station has the access attribute
FORWARD.

Examples:

A data station may have the topology (10, 10, 10); let (5, 3, 8) always
be the actual position.

distance	new position	
X	(5, 3, 9)	
X (-5)	(5, 3, 3)	
X (4)	(5, 4, 2)	(*)
SKIP (2)	(5, 5, 1)	
SKIP (-1)	(5, 2, 1)	
PAGE	(6, 1, 1)	
PAGE (6)	(1, 1, 1)	(**)
PAGE (-4)	(1, 1, 1)	
ADV (2, 5, 1)	(7, 8, 9)	
ADV (1, 0)	(5, 4, 8)	
ADV (-3, -2, 1)	(2, 1, 9)	
ADV (1, 8, 0)	(7, 1, 8)	(***)

94

The sum of actual position and distance may not exceed the bounds of the topology (as done in *, ** and ***) except the data station has the attribute **STREAM** and/or **CYCLIC** . **STREAM** allows to exceed internal bounds (see * and ***) but not to exceed the bound of the highest dimension (see **). In this case the data station must have the attribute **CYCLIC** . **STREAM** and **CYCLIC** are default attributes. If a data station has the attribute **NOSTREAM** or **NOCYCL** , the corresponding bounds must not be exceeded.

7.5   Get and Put Statement

The get statement is to put in, the put statement is to put out data with transforming them from external, alpha-numerical representation on **ALPHIC** data station into internal representation and vice versa, resp. The transformation is controlled implicitly or explicitly by formats.

Example:

(1)   The text

⌣⌣⌣ARTICLE - NO :⌣⌣1234
⌣⌣⌣STOCK :⌣⌣⌣⌣⌣⌣⌣⌣567

shall be put out to a display.

Necessary definitions and statements in the problem division:

. . .
SPC DISPLAY **DATION INOUT ALPHIC DIM** (*, 20, 80) FORWARD
    CONTROL (ALL);
DCL (ARTNO , STOCK) FIXED (15);
. . .
PUT 'ARTICLE - NO :', ARTNO , 'STOCK :', STOCK TO DISPLAY
    BY X (3), A (11), X (2), F (4), SKIP, X (3), A (6), X (7), F (4);

(2) Two values are to be put out with standard format to a new page of a printer.

```
. . .
SPC PRINTER DATION OUT ALPHIC DIM ( * , 60 , 120 ) FORWARD
    CONTROL ( ALL );
DCL A FIXED (15),
      X FLOAT (15);
. . .

A := 5;
X := 2.33;
. . .
PUT TO PRINTER BY PAGE;
PUT A , X TO PRINTER BY LIST;
. . .
```

The output has the following layout:

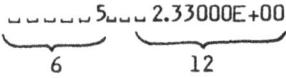

(3) Let some data be punched on cards with the following layout:

Column 1 - 10:   Article identification (CHARACTER)
Column 12 - 20:   Quantity (FIXED (15))
Column 22 - 30:   Price per unit, right aligned.

The data are to be read as values of the variables ARTIDENT ,
QUANT , PRICE.

. . .

SPC CARDREADER **DATION IN ALPHIC DIM** (* , 80) TFU
    FORWARD CONTROL (ALL);
DCL ARTIDENT CHAR (10) ,
    QUANT FIXED (15) ,
    PRICE FLOAT (15) ;
. . .

GET ARTIDENT , QUANT , PRICE FROM CARDREADER
    BY A (10) , X , F (9) , X , E (9) , SKIP ;
. . .

Generally the get and put statement have the following syntax:

    get-statement ::=
        GET (/ (name§variable / slice) , `` /)
        FROM name§dation (/ BY format-or-position , `` /) ;

    put-statement ::=
        PUT (/ (expression / slice) , `` /)
        TO name§dation (/ BY format-or-position , `` /) ;

    format-or-position ::=
        (/ mult /) (format / position)   /
        mult (format-or-position , ``)

    mult ::=
        (expression§which-yields-an-integer)

    format ::=
        simple-format / remote-format

    simple-format ::=
        F-format / E-format / A-format / B-format /
        T-format / D-format / list-format

97

When executing a get-statement the transfer items determined by position are put in one after another and assigned to the variables in the list of names and slices (list of variables). These assignments obey the general rules for assignments.

If an object of the list of variables is an array, then the determined transfer items are transferred line by line; if it is a structure, then the transfer items are assigned to the components of the structure corresponding to the sequence determined by the declaration of the structure (see III/1).

If the list of variables is omitted the list of formats and positions must be supplied.

In detail the procedure of executing a get-statement is as follows:

(1) Consider the first item in the list of formats and positions.

(2) . If it is a simple-format the first item in the list of variables is taken and it is checked, whether both items are compatible. (If the variable is an array or structure the first element of the array or structure is checked.) If they are compatible the data item determined by previous positioning is put in from the data station, transformed by the format and assigned to the variable.

. If it is a remote-format, the same procedure works analogously for the first simple-format in this remote-format.

. If it is a position the positioning is performed.

(3) Consider the next item in the list of formats and positions. Perform step (2) with "next" instead of "first".

(4) If the list of formats and positions is exhausted before the end of the list of variables is reached, then the list of formats and positions is processed again from the beginning except for the case, that it only contains positions.

(5) If the list of variables is exhausted, the list of formats and positions
is processed by executing the remaining positions until the next
format or the end of the list is found. Then the execution of the
get-statement is finished.

These rules apply analogously to the put-statement.

The data station in question must have the attribute **ALPHIC**, a topology,
an access attribute and the attribute **CONTROL** (ALL) , which means,
that compatibility checks have to be performed for all formats and positions. The access attribute may restrict the possibilities of positioning.

The list of formats and positions may contain multiplication factors in
order to write only once repeatedly occurring however identical terms.

Example:

X (2) , F (6, 2) , X (2) , F (6, 2) , X (2) , F (8, 2)

is equivalent to

(2) (X (2) , F (6, 2)) , X (2) , F (8, 2)

The following table defines the compatibility of formats and variables:

format	type
F-format	FIXED , FLOAT
E-format	FIXED , FLOAT
B-format	BIT
A-format	CHARACTER
T-format	CLOCK
D-format	DURATION
list-format	all these six types

Now the semantics of the different formats will be explained.

99

7.5.1 F-Format

F-format ::=

    F (width (/ , decim (/ , scale /) /))

width ::=

    expression§yielding-an-integer

declm ::=

    expression§yielding-an-integer

scale ::=

    expression§yielding-an-integer

The F-format defines the external representation of decimal fixpoint numbers. The width w denotes the total number of alphanumerical symbols needed to represent the decimal number (including preceding or succeeding blanks). Decim d denotes the number of decimal digits after the decimal point. The decimal digits preceding the decimal point are given by the value of the transfer item after multiplication by $10 ** s$ (in case of output) or $10 ** (-s)$ (in case of input).
F (w) and F (w, d) are defaulted to F (w, 0, 0) and F (w, d, 0) , respectively.

Output

The value of the object in the list of expressions and slices is put out right aligned to a field of length w in the following form:

    (/⌴ ··· /) (/ + / - /) digit ··· (/ . digit ··· /)

In the case of F (w, 0, 0) only the integer part of the value of the object is put out (rounding according to DIN 1333 implied) in the form:

    (/⌴ ··· /) (/ + / - /) digit ···

Leading zeros are replaced by blanks except for one zero, if the integer part is zero after rounding.

If the value of the object cannot be represented within w alphanumerical symbols, w asterisks are put out.

If w <= 0 no symbol is put out; the object in the list of expressions and slices is skipped.

Input

The external representation must consist of w symbols:

$$(/\text{␣} \cdots /) \ (/ \ (/ + / - /) \ \text{digit} \cdots \ (/ \ . \ (/ \text{digit} \cdots /) \ /) \ /) \ (/\text{␣} \cdots /)$$

If all symbols are blanks the value is defaulted to zero.

If the sequence doesn't contain a decimal point, the rightmost d digits are interpreted as digits after the decimal point. In this case, s must be greater than or equal to d.

If the sequence contains a decimal point, d is overridden.

If w <= 0 no assignation is made; the corresponding object is skipped.

Examples:

value	format	output
13.5	F (7, 2)	␣␣13.50
275.2	F (4, 5)	* * * *
22.8	F (5)	␣␣␣23
212.73	F (9, 2, 2)	␣21273.00
212.73	F (9, 2)	␣␣␣212.73

7.5.2 E-Format

E-format ::=
      E (width (/ , decim (/ , significance /) /))

significance ::=
      expression§yielding-an-integer

The E-format defines the external representation of decimal floating point numbers. Width and decim have the same meaning as the F-format, significance denotes the number of significant digits of the mantissa.

Output

E (w, d) is defaulted to E (w, d, d+1), E (w) is defaulted to E (w, 0, 1).

The value of the object in question is put out right aligned to a field of length w in the following form:

    (/␣$^{...}$ /) (/ + / - /) digit $^{...}$. (/ digit $^{...}$ /) E (+ / -) digit digit

The exponent is determined such that the leading digit of the mantissa is different from zero, if the value of the object is different from zero. In case of d = 0 this implies w >= 6 for positive numbers and w >= 7 for negative numbers.

If w is too small to put out any digit of the mantissa a sequence of w asterisks is put out.

If w <= 0 no symbol is put out; the corresponding object is skipped.

If 0 < w > d > s the mantissa is determined such that

$$10^{2-d-1} <= |\,\text{mantissa}\,| < 10^{s-d}$$

The floating point number must be represented in one of the possible
forms of simple real constant denotation (see part I/ 2.2.2). It may be
located anywhere within a field of length w; preceding and succeeding
blanks are ignored.

Since here the parameter significance doesn't mean anything the same
rules as for input with F-format apply analogously.

Examples:

value	format	output
-0.07	E (9, 1)	-7.0E-02
2713.5	E (11, 2, 4)	27.13E+02
2721	E (8)	2.E+03

7.5.3 A-Format

A-format ::=
  A (/ (width) /)

The A-format defines the external representation of character strings.
The width w has the same meaning as in 7.5.1.

Output

If w is omitted then w is set to the length lg of the value of the CHARACTER
object in question. This value is put out left-aligned to a field of length w
in the form:

(character-without-apostrophe / ') $\cdots$ (/␣ $\cdots$ /)

If lg > w then lg - w characters are lost to the right.

If lg < w then w - lg blanks are added to the right.

If w = 0 no symbol is put out and the object is skipped.

Width w must not be omitted.

Width characters are read and assigned to the **CHARACTER** variable
in question, which may have the length lg.

If w < lg then lg - w blanks are added to the right.

If w > lg then the characters in excess are lost (right truncation).

If w = 0 no assignation is made and the variable is skipped.

Examples:

Putting out the character string ' PEARL ' with format

- A (5)   yields   PEARL
- A (7)   yields   PEARL ⌴⌴
- A (2)   yields   PE

Putting in the character string ' PEARL ⌴⌴' to a variable TEXT
of type **CHAR** (5) with format

- A (5) is equivalent to   TEXT := ' PEARL ';
- A (7) is equivalent to   TEXT := ' PEARL ';
- A (2) is equivalent to   TEXT := ' PE⌴⌴⌴';

7.5.4   B-Format

B-format ::=
     (B / B1 / B2 / B3 / B4) (/ (width) /)

The B-format defines the external representation of values of **BIT** objects.
The width w has the same meaning as in 7.5.1.

Output

If w is omitted w is set to the length lg of the value of the **BIT** object
in question. This value is put out left aligned to a field of length w in
the form:

Bl-digit ⋯ (/⎵ ⋯ /) in case of B / Bl-format
B2-digit ⋯ (/⎵ ⋯ /) in case of B2-format
B3-digit ⋯ (/⎵ ⋯ /) in case of B3-format
B4-digit ⋯ (/⎵ ⋯ /) in case of B4-format

If $lg > w$ then $lg - w$ bits are lost to the right.

If $lg < w$ then $w - lg$ zeros are added to the right.

If $w = 0$ no symbol is put out and the object is skipped.

Input

Width w must be supplied.

A field of length w is read, which must contain a bit string in the form

B4-digit ⋯

Preceding or succeeding blanks are ignored. The rules for input with A-format apply analogously. (Replace blank by zero.)

Examples:

Putting out the bit string '0101110'B with format

.   B (5)   yields   01011
.   B2 (3)   yields   113
.   B3   yields   270
.   B4 (2)   yields   5C

Let BITSTRING be a variable of type **BIT** (8) in the following input examples:

input string	format	value of BITSTRING
11111	B (5)	11111000
201	B2 (3)	10000100
235	B3 (3)	01001110
AB	B4 (2)	10101011

T-format ::=
    T (width (/ , decim /))

The T-format defines the external representation of values of **CLOCK** objects. The width w has the same meaning as in 7.5.1, decim d denotes the number of decimal digits after the decimal point. T (w) is defaulted to T (w, 0).

Output

The value of the **CLOCK** object in question is put out right aligned to a field of length w in the form:

(/␣ ··· /) (/ digit /) digit : digit digit : digit digit (/ . digit ··· /)

The leading digit is replaced by a blank if it equals zero.

If d = 0 the decimal point and the following digits are not put out.

Input

A field of length w is read which must contain a valid clock constant denotation anywhere in the field. Preceding or succeeding blanks are ignored.

Examples:

value	format	output
12.30 a.m. 5.2 sec	T (12, 1)	␣␣12:30:5.2
8 a.m.	T (8)	␣ 8:00:00

7.5.6 D-Format

D-format ::=
        D (width (/ , decim /))

The D-format defines the external representation of values of
DURATION objects. Width w and decim d have the same meaning as
in 7.5.5. D (w) is defaulted to D (w, 0).

Output

The value of the **DURATION** object in question is put out right
aligned in a field of length w in the form

   (/␣ ··· /) (/ digit /) digit HRS digit digit MIN digit digit (/ . digit ··· /) SEC

The leading digit is replaced by a blank if it equals zero.
If d = 0 the decimal point and following digits are not put out.

Input

A field of length w is read which must contain a valid duration constant
denotation anywhere in the field. Preceding or succeeding blanks are
ignored.

Examples:

value	format	output
11 hours and 15 minutes	D (20)	11␣HRS␣15␣MIN␣00␣SEC
100 milli- seconds	D (24, 3)	␣0␣HRS␣00␣MIN␣00.100␣SEC

7.5.7 List-Format

List-format ::=

LIST

The list-format can be used to put in or to put out values of **FIXED**, **FLOAT**, **BIT**, **CHAR**, **CLOCK** and **DURATION** objects by means of standard formats.

Output

Subsequent data are separated by two blanks, respectively.

The following table shows the attachment between types and standard formats, i.e. the value of an object of one of these types is put out as if the attached format would be its corresponding format in a put statement.

Type	standard format
CHAR (k)	A (k)
BIT (k)	B (k)
FIXED (k)	F (m)
FLOAT (k)	E (n, n-7, 8)
CLOCK	T (8)
DUR	D (20)

with $m = $ ENTIER $(k/3.32) + 2$ and $n = $ ENTIER $(k/3.32) + 8$.

Input

The input data may have any valid representation described in paragraphs 7.5.1 to 7.5.6. They have to be separated by a comma or at least two blanks, respectively. If there isn't any data between two commas, the corresponding object in the list of variables is skipped without assignment.

Examples:

type	value	standard format	output
FIXED (15)	127	F (6)	127
FLOAT (15)	3.28E+28	E (12, 5, 8)	3.28000E+28
BIT (8)	'EF'B4	B (8)	11101111

7.5.8 Remote-Format

Often identical lists of formats and positions have to be used in several
get or put statements. Then the remote-format allows to write this list
only once and to attach an identifier to it (in a remote-format-declaration) in order to use only this identifier in the different I/O statements.

> remote-format-declaration ::=
>   identifier : **FORMAT** (format-or-position , ") ;

Remote-formats must be declared at module level. They can be referred
to in get and put statements at the position of remote-format by denoting
their identifier in the following form:

> remote-format ::=
>   R (identifier§format)

Example:

> FTAB : **FORMAT** (X (2) , F (8, 3) , (3) (X (2) , E (10, 3))) ;
> . . .
> **PUT** A , X , Y , Z **TO** PRINTER **BY** R (FTAB) ;
> . . .

The list of formats and positions in the remote-format-declaration must
not contain any remote-format referring directly or indirectly to this
remote-format-declaration.

7.6   Take and Send Statement

The take statement is to put in, the send statement is to put out process
control data from or to data stations having the attribute **BASIC** .

Generally the data are transferred without transformation.

If necessary, special formats could be implemented and used analogously
to the standard formats and positions.

take-statement ::=
  TAKE (/ (name§variable / slice) , ·· /)
  FROM name§dation (/ **BY** format-or-position , ·· /) ;

send-statement ::=
  SEND (/ (expression / slice) , ·· /)
  TO name§dation (/ **BY** format-or-position , ·· /) ;

Since no standard formats or positions should be used, the same rules
as for read and write statements apply analogously.

Example:

  The task MONITOR has to take the actual status of a device. Then
  it has to start a motor by putting out '1'B.

  MODULE (EXAMPLE) ;

  SYSTEM ;
  DEVICE : DIGIN (2) * 2, 8 ;
  MOTOR : DIGOUT (1) * 7 ;

  PROBLEM ;
  SPC DEVICE **DATION IN BASIC** ,
   MOTOR **DATION OUT BASIC** ;

  MONITOR : **TASK** ;
   DCL STATUS **BIT** (8) ;
   . . .
   TAKE STATUS **FROM** DEVICE ;
   . . .
   SEND '1'B **TO** MOTOR ;
   . . .
   END ;
  . . .
  MODEND ;

Part III

Additional Possibilities

1. STRUCTURES

Scalar variables of the <u>same</u> type will be summarized to an array with one identifier; the various variables are referred to by this identifier and their index.

However, many technical processes - specially those with dispositive character, require to describe data structures with components of <u>different</u> types.

Example:

The transmissions of a daily TV news broadcasting are stored in a magnetic tape device.
The sequence of a specific news broadcasting is disposed by editors with the aid of a computer controlling the magnetic tape devices. For each broadcasting a data record is required - possessing e.g. the following structure

. Identity of broadcasting
. Archives number
. Information, if this broadcasting was already transmitted in the first, second or third news broadcasting of the day
. Start position of transmission on tape
. End position of transmission on tape
. Information, if original sound is available
. Length of speaker's text
. Text - possibly to be used by news speaker

Such data structures can be described problem orientedly as structures. In above mentioned example the following applies:

```
DCL TRANSMISSION STRUCT
    [ ( IDENTITY, ARCHIVES ) FIXED ,
    ALREADYBROADCASTED (3) BIT (1) ,
    ( START, STOP ) FIXED ,
    ORIGINALSOUND BIT (1) ,
    TEXTLENGTH FIXED ;
    TEXT CHAR (200) ] ;
```

A structure is always set in brackets.

Different to elements of arrays, components of a structure are not referred to by their common identifier and an index; however, they are referred to by their common identifier and the identifier they have been given in their declaration, whereby the two identifiers are divided by a point.

Example:

By execution of the statement

TRANSMISSION.START := 1027 ;

the component START of structure TRANSMISSION receives the value 1027.

As the declaration of TRANSMISSION shows, components are allowed to be arrays. As usual array elements are referred to by their identifier and index, which in turn follows the identifier of the structure:

IF TRANSMISSION.ALREADYBROADCASTED (1) **THEN ... FIN ;**

The components of structures can as well be structures, whereby not only linear but also hierarchical data structures can be described.

Example:

A data set of persons contains information of the employees; each description may have the following structure:

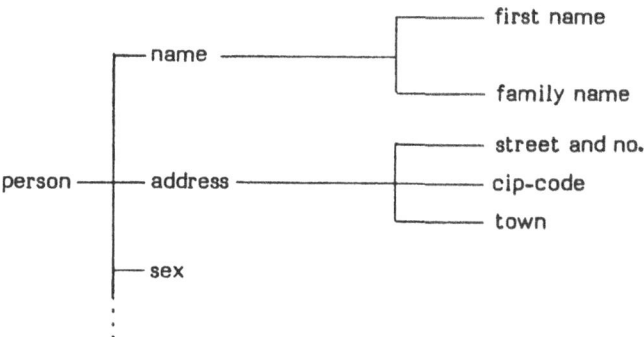

The components name and address are themselves structures, namely substructures of the main structure person.

```
DCL PERSON STRUCT
      [NAME STRUCT
            [FIRSTNAME CHAR (10) ,
             FAMILYNAME CHAR (15)
            ] ,
       ADDRESS STRUCT
             [STREET CHAR (15) ,
              CIPCODE FIXED ,
              TOWN CHAR (15)
             ] ,
       SEX CHAR (1)
       . . .
      ] ;
   . . .
```

Summarizing components into substructures is useful e.g. in connection
with I/O statements. In case only name and address of a person shall
be printed the following statement applies (see II/ 7.5).

> PUT PERSON.NAME, PERSON.ADDRESS TO PRINTER
> BY A (10), (2) (X (2), A (15)), X (2), F (4), X (1), A (15) ;

Substructures can be denoted by their identifiers preceded by the names
of higher-ranked structures.

The type of a structure is determined by the arrangement of its components
and their types. Structures of the same type can be composed to arrays:

> DCL TRANSMISSION (20) STRUCT . . . ; /* SEE ABOVE */

In general the component of a structure is referred to by its identifier
(possibly followed by an index) and the identifiers of higher-ranked components (each possibly followed by an index), whereby these names
are divided by points and whereby names of higher-ranked components
precede those of lower-ranked components.

Example:

> PERSON.NAME.FIRSTNAME := 'JOHN' ;
> IF TRANSMISSION(1).ALREADYBROADCASTED(J) THEN ... FIN ;

114

Now the phrase "name" can be defined in generalising the definition
of part II/ 5.1:

name ::=
    identifier ((/ (index , ˮ) /)) . ˮ

Examples:

    A , A (3) , A (I, J, 2*K) , A.B , A.B.C , A (3).B.C (I, J)

The identifiers of the components of a structure can be chosen independently
of identifiers outside of this structure:

DCL PERSON **STRUCT** ... , /* SEE ABOVE */
    TOWN **CHAR** (15) ;

    . . .

    PERSON.ADDRESS.TOWN := TOWN ;

In general structures have to be declared as follows:

structure-declaration ::=
    (DECLARE / DCL)
    (one-identifier-or-list§main-structure (/ bound-list /)
      structure-mode (/ resident-attribute /) (/ global-attribute /)
) , ˮ ;

structure-mode ::=
    identifier§user-defined-mode /
    STRUCT [((/ one-identifier-or-list§structure-component /)
                mode-in-structure-mode) , ˮ]

mode-in-structure-mode ::=
    (/ bound-list /) (simple-mode / structure-mode / reference-mode)

Identifier§user-defined-mode and reference-mode are explained in III/3
and III/4. Resident-attribute and global-attribute are described in III/9
and III/6.

115

Structures may occur as parameters of procedures. In this case they
have to be specified with **IDENT** .

Example:

    DCL COORDINATE **STRUCT**
        [X **BIT** (8) , Y **BIT** (5) , Z **BIT** (3)];
    . . .

    OUTPUT : **PROC** (DEVICENO **FIXED** ,
                    S **STRUCT** [X **BIT** (8) , Y **BIT** (5) , Z **BIT** (3)] **IDENT**);
            SEND S.X >< S.Y >< S.Z **TO** DEVICE (DEVICENO);
            END ;
    . . .
    CALL OUTPUT (I, COORDINATE);

Assignments between structures and substructures are allowed, if they
have the same type.

Example:

    DCL PERSON **STRUCT** ..., /* SEE ABOVE */
            NAME **STRUCT**
                [PRENAME **CHAR** (10) ,
                  FAMILY **CHAR** (15)
            ];
    . . .
    NAME.PRENAME := 'JOHN' ;
    NAME.FAMILY   := 'JOHNSON' ;
    . . .
    PERSON.NAME := NAME ;
    . . .

2. USING BIT-STRINGS AND CHARACTER-STRINGS

The i-th bit of a bit string can be referred to by means of the standard name BIT (i), which is stated behind the name of the bit string, divided by a point. A bit string called B with the length lg is known as structure B, which as the only component possesses a one-dimensional array BIT of length lg, elements are of type BIT (1).

Analogously the i-th character of a character string Z can be referred to by Z.CHAR (i) or Z.CHARACTER (i).

Hereby the bits or characters of a bit string or character string are enumerated from left to right - beginning with 1.

Example:

```
DCL  BYTE BIT (8) ,
     B BIT (1) ,
     I FIXED ;

BYTE := '11101111'B ;
B := BYTE.BIT (4) ;              /* B HAS THE VALUE '0'B */
BYTE.BIT (2) := '0'B ;          /* BYTE HAS THE VALUE '10101111'B */
I := 8 ;
BYTE.BIT (I) := B ;             /* BYTE HAS THE VALUE '10101110'B */
```

Furthermore it is possible to refer to slices (substrings) of bit strings or character strings in an analogous manner. The general rule is:

```
string-selection ::=
    name§string . ( BIT / CHAR / CHARACTER )
        ( ( integer-constant-denotation (/ : integer-constant-denotation /) ) /
          ( identifier (/ : identifier + integer-constant-denotation /) )
        )
```

The identifiers have to agree with each other and have to denote a variable for integers.

Example:

A stacker crane is connected to 16 adjacently situated connection points of a digital input device. The connection points have the following meaning:

Connection points   1 - 8 : X-coordinate
Connection points   9 - 12 : Y-coordinate
Connection point   13 : Z-coordinate
Connection points   14 - 16 : additional parameters

After positioning the real position of the stacker crane is to be read and checked.

```
MODULE ;

SYSTEM ;
CRANE : DIGIN (1) * (1 : 16) ;

PROBLEM ;
SPC CRANE DATION IN BASIC ;
. . .
MONITOR : TASK ;
    DCL STATUS BIT (16) ,
        XCOORD BIT (8) , YCOORD BIT (4) , ZCOORD BIT (1) ;
    . . .
    positioning
    TAKE STATUS FROM CRANE ;
    XCOORD := STATUS.BIT (1 : 8) ;
    YCOORD := STATUS.BIT (9 : 12) ;
    ZCOORD := STATUS.BIT (13) ;
    check
    . . .
    END ;
. . .
```

This piece of code can be programmed more flexible by fixing the start-positions of the substrings XCOORD, YCOORD and ZCOORD in the variables STARTX, STARTY, STARTZ.

In the following piece of code the attributes **INV** (invariant) and **INIT** (initial) are used; they will be explained in III/8 and III/7.

```
MONITOR : TASK ;
    . . .
    DCL ( STARTX, STARTY, STARTZ ) INV FIXED INIT (1,9,13) ;
    . . .
    XCOORD := STATUS.BIT (STARTX : STARTX + 7) ;
    YCOORD := STATUS.BIT (STARTY : STARTY + 3) ;
    ZCOORD := STATUS.BIT (STARTZ) ;
    . . .
    END ;
```

Assignments to substrings are also possible; in addition substrings may function as operands in expressions.

3.   DEFINITION OF NEW DATA TYPES

A specific structure can for example occur as parameter, as substructure
within another structure or as transfer-item-type of a data station.
In any of these cases the type of this structure has to be stated, which
requires much writing concerning structures of higher complexibility.
Therefore and for reasons of program readability the type of a structure
can be defined as new data type; the identifier of this new data type
can be choosen freely. After definition this identifier can be used to
declare or specify variables having the new type.

Example:

```
PROBLEM ;
. . .
TYPE NEWS STRUCT
     [(IDENTITY, ARCHIVES) FIXED ,
      ALREADYBROADCASTED (3) BIT (1) ,
      (START, STOP) FIXED ,
      ORIGINALSOUND BIT (1) ,
      TEXTLENGTH FIXED ,
      TEXT CHAR (200)
     ];

DCL SETOFNEWS DATION INOUT NEWS . . . ;

COORDINATION : TASK ;
     DCL TRANSMISSION NEWS ;
     . . .
     READ TRANSMISSION FROM SETOFNEWS ;
     . . .
     END ;
. . .
```

Additional examples for user defined data types are described in connection with reference variables (III/4).

Generally a new data type is defined as follows:

type-definition ::=
      TYPE identifier§new-data-type   structure-mode ;

New data types must be defined at module level; they can be used at module level and in all tasks and procedures of this module. In order to use them in other modules they have to be defined in these modules too.

4. INDIRECT ADDRESSING WITH REFERENCE-VARIABLES

In PEARL, indirect addressing is possible by using so-called reference
variables (pointer variables). Contrary to the variables already introduced,
reference variables do not have problem or control data as values, but
the names of variables (reference variables refer (point) to variables).
Analogously to other variables the range of a reference variable is limited
to one type of variables, which has to be stated when declaring it.

The value of a reference value (the referenced variable) can be referred
to by means of the monadic operator **CONT**; this operation is called
"dereferencing".

Examples:

```
    DCL ( K, L ) FIXED ,
        X FLOAT ,
        ( RK1, RK2 ) REF FIXED ,      /* FIXED-REFERENCE-VAR */
        RX REF FLOAT ;                /* FLOAT-REFERENCE-VAR */
    RK1 := K ;              /* RK1 GETS THE VALUE K OR
                               'RK1 'POINTS' TO K */
    RK1 := L ;             /* RK1 POINTS TO L */
    RK2 := RK1 ;           /* RK2 POINTS TO L */
    RX := X ;              /* RX POINTS TO X */
    RX := K ;              /* WRONG: K HAS NOT TYPE FLOAT */
    RX := RK1 ;            /* WRONG: RK2 HAS NOT TYPE REF FLOAT */
    L := 2 ;
    K := CONT RK1 ;        /* K = 2 */
    RK2 := 3 ;             /* WRONG: 3 IS NO VARIABLE */
    CONT RK2 := 3 ;        /* L = 3 */
    CONT RK2 := K ;        /* L = 2 */
```

Instead of K := **CONT** RK1 simply K := RK1 can be used, i.e. the
operator **CONT** can be skipped at the right side of an assignment ("implicit
dereferencing").

Generally the following rule applies:

    reference-declaration ::=
        (DECLARE / DCL) one-identifier-or-list (/ bound-list /)
        reference-mode (/ resident-attribute /) (/ global-attribute /) ;

    reference-mode ::=
        REF (/ virt-bound-list /)
        (simple-mode / structure-mode / dation-mode / SEMA / BOLT /
        IRPT / INTERRUPT / SIGNAL)

    dereferencing ::=
        CONT name§reference-variable

The definition of reference-mode shows the types of variables, to which
reference variables are allowed to point. Especially, reference variables
must not point to reference variables. They are, however, permitted
to point to arrays and structures, which in turn may have reference
variables as elements or components. This possibility can be used to
link structures or in general to construct lists.

Example:

    A task controls certain devices; another task is providing the con-
    trol orders independently, i.e. at one time more than one order
    may exist. Therefore and because of their different priorities the
    orders are büffered in a queue ORDERQUEUE . Each order may
    have the user defined type ORDERTYPE ; this type shall also
    contain the priority of the order, which is used to enqueue new
    orders. The reference variables NEXTORDER and FREE point
    to the next order and to the next free space in the queue ORDER-
    QUEUE ; starting with FREE all free spaces shall be linked to-
    gether. ORDERQUEUE shall have at last 10 elements.

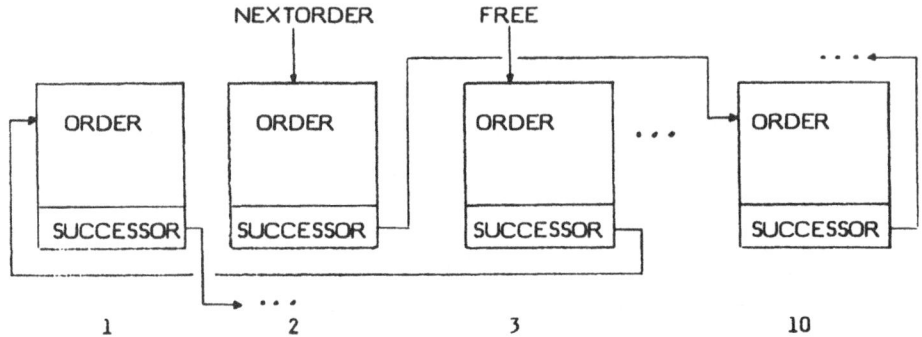

ORDERQUEUE can be declared as follows:

```
...

TYPE QUEUEELEMENT STRUCT
     [ ORDER ORDERTYPE ,
       SUCCESSOR REF QUEUEELEMENT ];

DCL ORDERQUEUE (10) QUEUEELEMENT ,
     ( NEXTORDER, FREE ) REF QUEUEELEMENT ;

...
```

After initialisation and after having enqueued several orders an executed
order can be dequeued e.g. by the call of a self-made procedure DEQUEUE :

```
DEQUEUE : PROCEDURE ;
         DCL HELP REF QUEUEELEMENT ;
         HELP := NEXTORDER ;
         NEXTORDER := NEXTORDER.SUCCESSOR ;
         HELP.SUCCESSOR := FREE ;
         FREE := HELP ;
         END ;
```

These statements are additional examples for implicit dereferencing:

In case a reference-variable R points to an array A with the elements
A (i, j, k, ...) or to a structure S with the components S.Ci, the elements
of A or components of S can be referred to by R (i, j, k, ...) or R.Ci without using CONT .

Furthermore a reference variable R is implicitly dereferenced,

- if R is actual parameter of a procedure call and if the corresponding formal parameter is not a reference variable,
- if R is operand of a dyadic operator which is not defined for
  values of reference variables like **IS** (see below).

Example:

```
...
DCL R REF FIXED ,
    K FIXED ;
R := K ;
K := 2 ;
K := R + 1 ;          /* EQUIVALENT K := K + 1 ; */
```

In order to indicate for example the end of a queue the reference variable
NIL can be used, which has a certain constant value. Consequently the
above mentioned ORDERQUEUE can be initialized as follows:

```
FOR I TO 9 REPEAT
    ORDERQUEUE (I).SUCCESSOR := ORDERQUEUE ( I + 1 );
    END ;
ORDERQUEUE (10).SUCCESSOR := NIL ;
```

Values of reference variables can be compared by means of the dyadic
operators **IS** and **ISNT**; the result of **IS** (**ISNT**) is 'l'B, if its operands,
reference variables, have the same (different) values, otherwise the
result is '0'B.

Example:

```
IF NEXTORDER IS NIL THEN ... FIN ;
```

125

5. BLOCK STRUCTURE, SCOPE OF OBJECTS

Blocks are used to structure the bodies of tasks and procedures and to influence the scope and lifetime of PEARL objects (data, procedures, etc.). A block is a comprehension of declarations and statements:

> block ::=
>   **BEGIN** (/ declaration ''' /) (/ statement ''' /) **END** ;

Blocks are statements; therefore they may be used only within bodies of tasks and procedures. Blocks may be nested. A block is entered by execution of **BEGIN** ; the block is left by execution of the corresponding **END** or by execution of a jump to a label outside of the block. Jumps into a block are forbidden.

When entering a block, storage is allocated for the objects declared within the block ('local' objects). This storage is given free when leaving the block. Consequently blocks can be used like tasks, procedures and loop statements to introduce and to remove objects dynamically, i.e. to use the given storage for different objects.

Therefore several rules for the scope and lifetime of these objects must be observed:

The lifetime of an object is the (execution) time between the execution of its declaration and the execution of the end of the block (or loop statement or procedure or task or module), where the declaration is made.

Example:

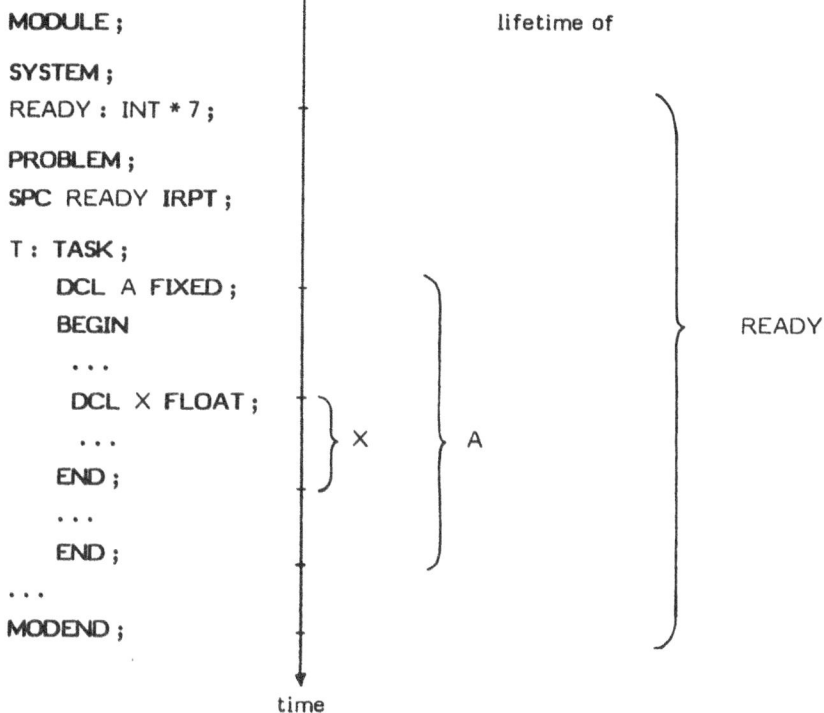

The scope of an object consists of all parts of a program where this object can be used (referred to). The following rules have to be observed:

- If an object is declared at module level, it can be used at module level and within all tasks and procedures of this module (see however III/6) and within all nested procedures, blocks and loop statements with the following exception: it cannot be used within those tasks and procedures, where another object is declared with the same name.

- If an object is declared within a task, procedure, loop statement or block, it can be used within this task, procedure, loop statement or block and within all enclosed procedures, loop statements or blocks with the following exception: it cannot be used within those enclosed procedures, loop statements or blocks, where another object is declared with the same name.

Therefore it is possible, to choose the names of local objects within blocks independently of the environment of the block. In other words, existing blocks may be integrated into programs without conflicts concerning names.

Example:

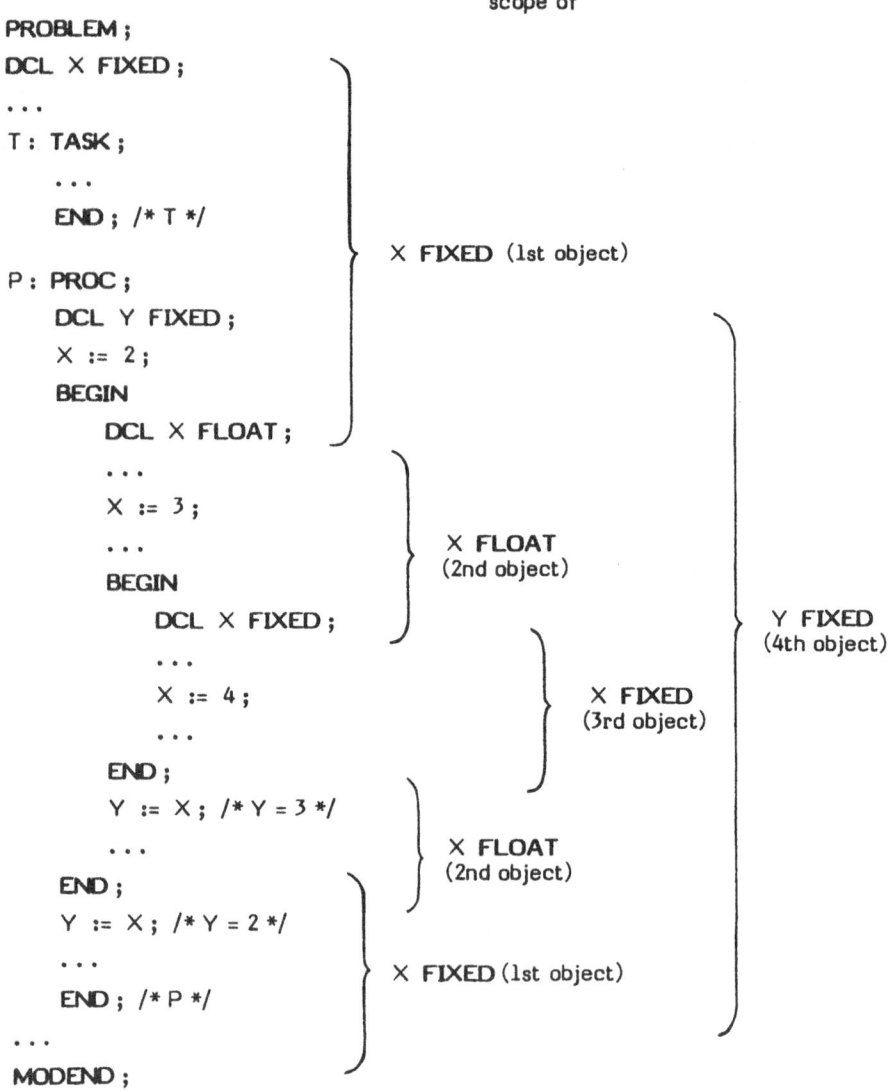

```
                                              scope of
PROBLEM ;
DCL X FIXED ;
...
T : TASK ;
    ...
    END ; /* T */
                                    X FIXED (1st object)
P : PROC ;
    DCL Y FIXED ;
    X := 2 ;
    BEGIN
        DCL X FLOAT ;
        ...
        X := 3 ;
        ...                         X FLOAT
        BEGIN                       (2nd object)
            DCL X FIXED ;
            ...                                          Y FIXED
            X := 4 ;                     X FIXED         (4th object)
            ...                          (3rd object)
        END ;
        Y := X ; /* Y = 3 */
        ...                         X FLOAT
    END ;                           (2nd object)
    Y := X ; /* Y = 2 */
    ...                             X FIXED (1st object)
    END ; /* P */
...
MODEND ;
```

128

6. COMMUNICATION BETWEEN MODULES

In case an object shall be used in several modules of a program, it has
to be declared (i.e. allocated) with the global attribute at module level
of one module and to be specified with the global attribute at module
level of all other modules. Taking into consideration the scope rules
of the preceding paragraph the scope of such a 'global' object consists
of all modules, where it is declared or specified.

Example:

```
    MODULE ;                    |    MODULE ;
    PROBLEM ;                   |    PROBLEM ;
        . . .                   |        . . .
        DCL X FIXED GLOBAL ;    |        SPC X FIXED GLOBAL ;
        X := 2 ;                |        X := 3 ;
        . . .                   |        . . .
    MODEND ;                    |    MODEND ;
```

All data stations, interrupts and signals, which are listed in the system
division of a certain module, are implicitly declared with the global
attribute. Therefore they are specified in all problem divisions, where
they shall be used. The global attribute may be omitted in the specifications of the module, where they are declared in the system division.

The optionally stated identifier of a module (see II/1) extends implicitly
the names of the module. Caused by this fact it is possible to declare
different global objects in different modules with the same name; to
use one of these objects in another module it is specified by stating its
name together with the module identifier.

Example:

```
    MODULE (Ml) ;                            MODULE (M2) ;

    SYSTEM ;                                 PROBLEM ;
    READY (1:10) : INT * (2:11) ;            DCL X FIXED GLOBAL ;

    PROBLEM ;                                . . .
    SPC READY ( ) IRPT ;                     MODEND ;
    DCL X FIXED GLOBAL ;

    . . .

    MODEND ;
```

```
    MODULE ;

    PROBLEM ;
    SPC READY ( ) IRPT GLOBAL ,
        X FIXED GLOBAL (Ml) ;  /* X OF Ml */

    . . .

    MODEND ;
```

The general forms of the global-attribute and specification are as follows:

```
    global-attribute ::=
        GLOBAL (/ ( identifier§module ) /)


    specification ::=
        ( SPECIFY / SPC )
        ( one-identifier-or-list
          ( spc-attribute /
            proc-spc-attribute /
            task-spc-attribute )
        ) , ¨ ;


    spc-attribute ::=
        (/ virt-bound-list /)
        ( simple-mode / structure-mode / reference-mode / SEMA /
          BOLT / INTERRUPT / IRPT / SIGNAL / dation-mode )
        (/ resident-attribute /) (/ global-attribute /)
```

```
proc-spc-attribute ::=
    procedure-mode
    (/ resident-attribute /) (/ reentrant-attribute /) global-attribute

procedure-mode ::=
    ENTRY
    (/ ( ( (/ virt-bound-list /) parameter-mode (/ IDENTICAL / IDENT /) )," ) /)
    (/ result-attribute /)

task-spc-attribute ::=
    TASK  (/ resident-attribute /) global-attribute
```

Example:

```
MODULE ;                              MODULE ;
PROBLEM ;                             PROBLEM ;
T : TASK PRIO 3 GLOBAL ;              SPC T TASK GLOBAL ,
    task-body                             P ENTRY ( (,) FIXED IDENT )
    END ;                                 GLOBAL ;
P : PROC ( A (,) FIXED IDENT )        INITIALISATION : TASK ;
    GLOBAL ;                              DCL M (10,20) FIXED ;
    procedure-body                        . . .
    END ;                                 CALL P (M) ;
. . .                                     . . .
MODEND ;                                  ACTIVATE T ;
                                          . . .
                                          END ;
                                      . . .
                                      MODEND ;
```

131

The spc-attribute defines, which objects may be global. The global attribute may be omitted only in the specification of those data stations, interrupts and signals, which are declared in the system division of the same module.

The specification of an object must contain all attributes of the declaration of this object except its length or precision. In this exceptional case the length or precision in the extended scope is that of the length definition (see III/15) of the module, where the object is specified.

Resident attribute and reentrant attribute are explained in III/9 and III/10.

7. INITIAL ATTRIBUTE

The attribute **INITIAL** allows to preset the values of variables for problem data in their declaration. This initialisation is the only possibility
to assign values to variables which have the attribute **INV** (see III/8).
The attribute **INITIAL** has to be the last attribute in a declaration.

> initial-attribute ::=
>   (**INITIAL / INIT**) (((/ + / - /) constant-denotation) , ″)

The type of the constant denotations must be compatible with the type
of the declared variables (see II/5.2, assignment).

Arrays and structures may be initialised too. In case of an array initialisation the elements of the list of constant denotations are attached from
left to right to the elements of the array line by line, in case of a structure
initialisation they are attached to the components of the structure in the
order of the components. If an array or structure has more elements or
components than there are elements in the list of constant denotations
then the remaining elements or components of the array or structure
are initialised with the last constant denotation.

Example:

> DCL NUMBEROFDEVICES **FIXED INIT** (12) ,
>   (LOWERBOUND, UPPERBOUND) **FIXED INIT** (2, 15);

The values of NUMBEROFDEVICES, LOWERBOUND and UPPERBOUND
are 12, 2 and 15, according to the general rule, that the elements of a
list of constant denotations in the initial attribute correspond to the
elements of the identifier list in the written sequence.

> DCL TABLE (3 : 2) **FIXED INIT** (0, 1, -1);

TABLE (1, 1) has the value 0, TABLE (1, 2) has the value 1;
all other elements of TABLE have the value -1.

8. INVARIANT ATTRIBUTE

In order to protect variables for problem data from assignments (not
initialisations) these variables are declared with the attribute **INV**
immediately before the type attribute.

Example:

```
    . . .
    DCL PI INV FLOAT INIT (3.14159);
    . . .
    PI := 3;          /* ERROR */
```

If a variable is declared with the attribute **INV** , this protection must
not be removed. Therefore it has to be considered in all specifications
of this variable especially when using the variable as parameter of a
procedure and when using it as value of a reference variable. On the
other hand variables may be specified with the attribute **INV** without
being declared with the attribute **INV**; doing so the variable is protected
from assignments within the extended scope.

Example:

```
    . . .
    P : PROC ( A ( , ) INV FIXED IDENT , X FLOAT IDENT );
        procedure body
        END ;

    DCL TABLE (10, 20) FIXED ,
        PI INV FLOAT INITIAL (3.14159) ,
        R1 REF FLOAT ,
        R2 REF INV FLOAT ;
    . . .

    CALL P ( TAB, PI );      /* WRONG */
    R1 := PI ;               /* WRONG */
    R2 := PI ;
```

The call of P is wrong, because the formal parameter X (corresponding to the actual parameter PI) is not specified with the attribute **INV** . Therefore assignments to X (actually PI) would be possible in the body of P, i.e. the protection of PI would be removed.

Contrary to this the transfer of TAB to A in the same call is correct, because it doesn't restrict any protection but leads to a local protection of TAB within the body of P.

The assignment R1 := PI is wrong because otherwise the protection of PI could be removed by an (allowed) assignment to **CONT** R1. On the other hand the assignment R2 := PI would have been right even if PI would have been declared without the attribute **INV** .

9.   RESIDENT OBJECTS

Variables for problem data and control data may be declared and
specified with the attribute **RESIDENT** . This attribute signalizes that
the corresponding variable will be referred to frequently, which in general would require to keep the variable in a fast-access part of memory.

In general **RESIDENT** has no semantics in the usual sense; it essentially
permits certain optimizations at compiletime, thereby speeding up accesses
at runtime. If **RESIDENT** has a specific semantics in a specific implementation, this will be described in the user manual of this implementation.


```
resident-attribute  ::=
       RESIDENT
```

10. REENTRANT PROCEDURES

Procedures declared with the reentrant attribute can be used reentrant,
i.e. calling them simultaneously by several tasks (without explicit synchronization) never leads to conflicts in referring to local objects of these
procedures.

    reentrant-attribute ::=
        REENT

In the PEARL implementations of Werum all procedures declared at
module level are implicitly reentrant.

11. OPERATORS

11.1 Operators for Type Conversion

In an assignment generally the variable stated left of the assignment
symbol and the value of the expression stated right of the assignment symbol
must have the same type (see II/5.2). Especially only values of type
integer may be assigned to integer variables. In addition the types of
the operands of dyadic operators must be compatible (see II/5.1.2).

Therefore PEARL offers several operators for necessary type conversions.

The following table lists for each stated monadic operator

.   the type of its operand,

.   the type of its result and

.   its semantics.

In this table

.   a   represents any operand,

.   c   stands for the result of the operation,

.   p   stands for the precision and

.   lg stands for the length of the operands and results.

All listed operators are of precedence 1 (see II/5.1.3).

syntax	type of operand a	type of result c	semantics
TOFIXED a	CHAR (1)	FIXED (15)	c := integer associated to a by ASCII-code
	BIT (lg)	FIXED (p)	c := interpretation of a as integer with p = lg
TOFLOAT a	FIXED (p)	FLOAT (p)	c := a represented as a real number
TOBIT a	FIXED (p)	BIT (lg)	c := interpretation of a as bit-string with lg = p
TOCHAR a	FIXED	CHAR (1)	c := character associated to a by ASCII-code
ENTIER a	FLOAT (p)	FIXED (p)	c := nearest integer not greater than a
ROUND a	FLOAT (p)	FIXED (p)	c := nearest integer to a according to DIN 1333

Examples:

```
DCL  A FIXED (15) ,
     X FLOAT (15) ,
     (B, C) BIT (15) ;

. . .
A := ENTIER X/2 ;        /* EQU.  A := (ENTIER X) /2 ; */
A := ENTIER (X/2) ;
C := TOBIT A AND B ;
A := ROUND X + TOFIXED B ;
```

The precision of the result of an addition, subtraction, multiplication or division is the maximum of the precisions of both operands (see II/5.1.2). The dyadic operator FIT allows to fit the precision to the expected result.

syntax	type of a	type of b	type of the result
a FIT b	FIXED (p1)	FIXED (p2)	FIXED (p2)
	FLOAT (p1)	FLOAT (p2)	FLOAT (p2)

FIT changes the precision of a to the precision of b. It has the precedence 1.

Examples:

```
    . . .
    DCL  (A, B) FIXED (15) ,
          C FIXED (31) ;
    A := 65535 ;
    B := 2 ;
    C := A FIT C * B ;              /* C = 131070 */
```

11.2 Further Standard Operators

In addition to the operators presented in 11.1 and II/5.1 there exist by standard the monadic operators ABS, SIGN, LWB and UPB and the dyadic operators LWB and UPB. They are described by the following tables, where a and b stand for any operands, c for the result of the operations and p for the precision of operands and results.

All listed operators have the precedence 1.

Further monadic standard operators:

syntax	type of operand a	type of result c	semantics
ABS a	FIXED (p) FLOAT (p) DURATION	FIXED (p) FLOAT (p) DURATION	$c := \lvert a \rvert$ (absolute value)
SIGN a	FIXED (p) FLOAT (p) DURATION	FIXED (1)	$c := \begin{cases} +1 \text{ if } a > 0 \\ 0 \text{ if } a = 0 \\ -1 \text{ if } a < 0 \end{cases}$
LWB a	array	FIXED	$c :=$ lower bound of the first dimension of a
UPB a	array	FIXED	$c :=$ upper bound of the first dimension of a

Further dyadic standard operators:

syntax	type of operand a	type of operand b	type of result c	semantics
a LWB b	FIXED (p)	array	FIXED	$c :=$ lower bound of the a-th dimension of b, if it exists
a UPB b	FIXED (p)	array	FIXED	$c :=$ upper bound of the a-th dimension of b, if it exists

Example:

```
  . . .
P : PROC ( A ( , ) FIXED IDENT );
    . . .
    FOR I FROM LWB A TO UPB A REPEAT
        FOR K FROM 2 LWB A TO 2 UPB A REPEAT
            . . .
        END ;
    END ;
    . . .
    END ;
DCL TABLE1 (5, 10) FIXED ,
    TABLE2 (-1:2, 3:5) FIXED ;
. . .
CALL P (TABLE1);
. . .
CALL P (TABLE2);
    . . .
```

11.3   Definition of New Operators

The operator declaration described below is to define new operators
with freely choosable names or to change or to extend the semantics of
standard operators. This feature allows e.g. to extend the operators
+, -, . . . for complex numbers.

```
operator-declaration ::=
    OPERATOR op-name ( (/ op-parameter , /) op-parameter )
    result-attribute ;
    procedure-body
    END ;
```

142

op-name ::=

    identifier / + / - / * / / / ** / // / = / == / /= / < = / >= / < / > /< >/ ><

op-parameter ::=

    identifier (/ virt-bound-list /) parameter-mode (/ IDENTICAL / IDENT /)

Operators have to be declared at module level.

Example:

    The standard operator + shall be extended for complex numbers.

```
PROBLEM ;
TYPE COMPLEX STRUCT
      [REAL FLOAT , IMAG FLOAT];

OPERATOR + ( A COMPLEX IDENT , B COMPLEX IDENT )
              RETURNS (COMPLEX) ;
    DCL SUM COMPLEX ;
    SUM.REAL := A.REAL + B.REAL ;
    SUM.IMAG := A.IMAG + B.IMAG ;
    RETURN (SUM) ;
    END ;
DCL (XX, YY, ZZ) COMPLEX ,
    (X, Y, Z) FLOAT ;
...
ZZ := XX + YY ;
Z := X + Y ;
...
```

This example shows the possibility of defining different operations with
the same operator name, if the operands are of different type. When
evaluating an expression, where such an operator name occurs, that
operation is executed, whose parameter types are identical with the
types of the operands in the expression.

If a new operator has the name of a standard operator, this user defined
operator has the precedence of the standard operator. The precedence
of other new operators has to be defined with a precedence definition
before the operator declaration:

precedence-definition ::=
    PRECEDENCE op-name (1 / 2 / 3 / 4 / 5 / 6 / 7);

12.   INTERRUPT-STATEMENTS

Sometimes when a technical process is disturbed one wants to suppress
the reaction of an interrupt, i.e. the corresponding schedules of task
statements should remain invalid, when the interrupt occurs. This
can be achieved by execution of the disable statement; the counterpart
of the disable statement is the enable statement.

> disable-statement ::=
>   DISABLE name§interrupt ;

> enable-statement ::=
>   ENABLE name§interrupt ;

The scope of a disable-statement starts with its execution and ends with
the execution of an enable-statement.

Example:

```
MODULE ;
SYSTEM ;
ALARM : INT * 8 ;
. . .
PROBLEM ;
SPC ALARM INTERRUPT ;
. . .
START : TASK ;
    WHEN ALARM ACTIVATE ANALYSIS ;
    . . .
    END ;

ANALYSIS : TASK ;
    DISABLE ALARM ;
        analysis of the disturbance
        reaction
    ENABLE ALARM ;
    END ;
. . .
MODEND ;
```

Testing realtime programs off-line, it can be necessary to simulate
the occurrence of interrupts. This can be done with the help of the
trigger statement:

```
trigger-statement ::=
    TRIGGER name§interrupt ;
```

Example:

MODULE ;	MODULE (TEST) ;
SYSTEM ;	PROBLEM ;
READY : INT * 2 ;	SPC READY IRPT GLOBAL ;
. . .	. . .
PROBLEM ;	TRIGGER READY ;
SPC READY IRPT ;	(e.g. at random times)
. . .	
WHEN READY	. . .
ACTIVATE CONTROL ;	MODEND ;
. . .	
MODEND ;	

One problem in many discrete processes is to start the same task by
the occurrence of any of several interrupts of the same kind.

Example:

The task MONITOR shall be started if one of 20 possible interrupts of 20 switches in a conveyor system occurs. In order to react
right, MONITOR has to know the origin of the interrupt.

Problems like this can be solved by use of the standard function procedure
ORIGIN ; the result of ORIGIN is the index of that interrupt in an array
of interrupts, which has started the task, where ORIGIN is called.

Example:

```
MODULE ;
SYSTEM ;
SWITCH (1:8): INT * (1:8) ;
. . .
PROBLEM ;
SPC SWITCH ( ) IRPT ;

START : TASK ;
    WHEN SWITCH ACTIVATE MONITOR ;
    . . .
    END ;

MONITOR : TASK ;
    DCL I FIXED ;
    I := ORIGIN ;
        control of SWITCH (I)
    . . .
    END ;
. . .
MODEND ;
```

13.   SIGNALS

In contrast to interrupts, which represent external events, signals are
used to handle internal exceptional conditions arising during the execution of selected statements. Examples for signals are arithmetic
overflow, division by zero or end-of-file.

The set of possible signals is implementation dependent; it is described
in the special user manual of an implementation by listing the names
and semantics of the signals. Signals which are needed in a certain program have to be declared like interrupts in the system division, being
attached by freely chosen user names. They have to be specified in the
problem division with these user names at module level.

Example:

```
MODULE ;
SYSTEM ;
OVERFLOW : OFL ;        /* OFL shall be the system name */
ENDOFFILE : EOF ;       /* EOF  shall be the system name */
. . .
PROBLEM ;
SPC (OVERFLOW, ENDOFFILE) SIGNAL ;
. . .
MODEND ;
```

Generally signals have to be specified as follows:

```
signal-specification ::=
    ( SPECIFY / SPC ) one-identifier-or-list (/ ( ) /) SIGNAL
    (/ global-attribute /) ;
```

Arrays of signals are allowed.

The reaction to a signal is scheduled by the following statement:

```
schedule-for-signal-reaction ::=
    ON name§signal , " : unlabelled-statement
```

148

All unlabelled statements are allowed except a schedule-for-signal-reaction. Especially blocks or procedure calls are often convenient.

When one of the signals stated in the schedule-for-signal-reaction rises during the execution of a statement, the executing task stops the execution of this statement and executes the scheduled unlabelled statement. If this execution doesn't lead to a branch to another point of the program (e.g. by jump or termination), the task continues afterwards with the execution of the statement which follows the statement where the signal rised (analogously to a procedure call).

A schedule-for-signal-reaction is valid only within the task, procedure, loop statement or block, where it is stated. There, however, it is valid for all nested procedures, loop statements and blocks, if there are not stated other schedule-for-signal-reactions for the same signal.

Analogously to the trigger statement the induce statement allows to simulate the occurrence of a signal:

    induce-statement ::=
        INDUCE name§signal ;

Example:

    Every evening, the task EVALUATION has to evaluate a log file written during the day. The transfer units shall have the type EVENT.

149

...

PROBLEM ;

SPC ENDOFFILE SIGNAL ,
    TAPE DATION INOUT ALL ;

TYPE EVENT ...;

DCL LOGFILE DATION IN EVENT (*) FORWARD CREATED (TAPE);

EVALUATION : TASK ;
    DCL RECORD EVENT ;
    ...
    OPEN LOGFILE BY IDF ('LOG');
    ON ENDOFFILE : GOTO STOP ;
    ...
    READ RECORD FROM LOGFILE ;
    ...
STOP : CLOSE LOGFILE ;
    END ;

For test-purposes one could execute the statement

    INDUCE ENDOFFILE ;

instead of the read statement.

14. ADDITIONAL POSSIBILITIES IN THE SYSTEM DIVISION

The basic possibilities in the system division have been described in
paragraph II/7.1; now all possibilities to write a system division are
summarized:

> system-division ::=
>> **SYSTEM ;** (/ connection ··· /)

> connection ::=

$$
\text{connection-point } (/ \left\{ \begin{array}{c} \left\{ \begin{array}{c} -> \\ <- \\ <-> \end{array} \right\} \quad (/ \text{ connection-point } + \text{ ·· } /) \\[2em] + \text{ connection-point } + \text{ ·· } \end{array} \right\} /) ;
$$

> connection-point ::=
>> (/ user-name : /) ··· (/ system-name /)

$$
(/ * \left\{ \begin{array}{l} \text{identifier}\S\text{point} \\ \text{int}\S\text{point} \\ (\text{int} : \text{int } (/ \underline{/} \text{ int}\S\text{step } /) \underline{)} \end{array} \right\} (/ , \text{int}\S\text{width } /) /)
$$

> int ::=
>> integer-constant-denotation

> user-name ::=
>> identifier (/ (int : int) /)

> system-name ::=
>> identifier (/ (int (/ : int /)) /)

In addition to paragraph II/7.1 the following possibilities exist:

A device of the technical process can be connected with a group of devices
of the computer. E.G. a device with the user-name DEVICE shall be
connected with all 16 connection-points of the digital output device

DIGOUT (1) and with the connection points 2 - 4 of the digital output device DIGOUT (2) :

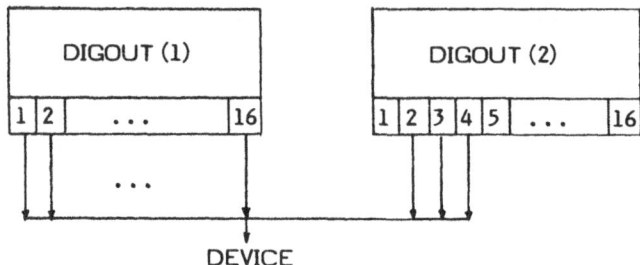

DEVICE

The corresponding description in the system division is

DEVICE : < - DIGOUT (1) * 1, 16 + DIGOUT (2) * 2, 3 ;

or

DEVICE : < - DIGOUT (1) * (1:16) + DIGOUT (2) * (2:4) ;

The elements of a group are combined by the symbol +.
This kind of description can also be used to describe not sequential connections:

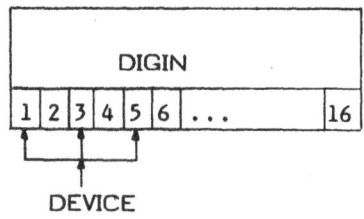

DEVICE

DEVICE :   -> DIGIN * 1 + DIGIN * 3 + DIGIN * 5 ;

Such connection can be described more simple by means of " / int§step", if the steps are equal as shown in this example:

DEVICE :   -> DIGIN * (1:5/2) ;

152

15. LENGTH DEFINITION

The length definition is to define the precision or length for those objects, whose precision or length is not defined by their (constant) denotation (see I/2.2) or declaration (see II/2.1).

length-definition ::=

    LENGTH
$$\left\{ \begin{array}{l} (\,\text{FIXED} \,/\, \text{FLOAT}\,) \;\underline{(\,\text{precision}\,)} \\ (\,\text{BIT} \,/\, \text{CHAR} \,/\, \text{CHARACTER}\,)\; \underline{(\,\text{length}\,)} \end{array} \right\} \; ;$$

Example:

```
PROBLEM ;
LENGTH FIXED (15) ;
LENGTH FLOAT (15) ;
DCL  A FIXED ,        /* A HAS  TYPE FIXED (15) */
     X FLOAT ,        /* X HAS  TYPE FLOAT (15) */
     Y FLOAT (31) ;   /* Y HAS  TYPE FLOAT (31) */
 . . .
```

Length definitions have to be stated at module level; they are valid for the whole module.

LITERATURE

Kappatsch 79   Kappatsch, A.; Mittendorf, H.; Rieder, P.: PEARL. Systema-
tische Darstellung für den Anwender. Oldenbourg, München -
Wien 1979.

Martin 78   Martin, T.: The Development of PEARL within the Process
Computer Control Project as Part of the 2nd and 3rd Data
Processing Programs of the Federal Government of Germany.
PDV-Bericht KFK-PDV 129, Kernforschungszentrum Karls-
ruhe GmbH, Status March 1978.

Martin 81   Martin, T.: PEARL at the Age of Five. Case Study of
Development and Application of a Common High Order
Realtime Programming Language. Computers in Industry,
Vol. 2, No. 1 (March 1981), p. 1 - 11.

Standard 78   DIN 66253 Teil 1: Basic PEARL . Entwurf 1978.
(English)

Standard 80   DIN 66253 Teil 2: Full PEARL . Entwurf 1980.
(English)

Steusloff 80   Steusloff, H.: Programming distributed computer systems
with higher level languages. In: Harrison, T.J. (Ed.): IFAC
Distributed Computer Control Systems, p. 39 - 50. Pergamon
Press, Oxford and New York 1980.

Syrbe 78   Syrbe, M.: Basic principles of advanced process control system
structures and a realization with optical fibres coupled distributed
microcomputers. IFAC 7th World Congress, June 1978, Helsinki,
p. 393 - 401. Pergamon Press, Oxford and New York 1978.

Werum 78   Werum, W.; Windauer, H.: PEARL . Beschreibung mit Anwen-
dungsbeispielen. Vieweg, Braunschweig 1978.

Appendix

1. LIST OF KEYWORDS WITH SHORT FORMS

The keywords not belonging to Basic PEARL are marked with an asterisk.
The numbers refer to the pages where the keywords are introduced.

ACTIVATE 42	* ENTER 54
AFTER 39	ENTRY 131
ALL 39, 82	
ALPHIC 81	FIN 68, 69
ALT 69	FIXED 22
AT 39	FLOAT 23
	FOR 71
BASIC 81	FORBACK 85
BEGIN 126	FORMAT 109
BIT 23	FORWARD 85
* BOLT 54	* FREE 54
BY 71, 85, 88	FROM 71, 88
CALL 32	GET 97
CASE 69	GLOBAL 129
CHARACTER , CHAR 24	GOTO 67
CLOCK 24	
CLOSE 87	HRS 11
* CONT 122	IDENTICAL, IDENT 31
CONTINUE 45	IF 68
CONTROL 85, 99	IN 80
CREATED 80	INDUCE 149
CYCLIC 95	INITIAL , INIT 133
	INOUT 80
DATION 79	INTERRUPT , IRPT 37
DECLARE , DCL 20	INV 134
DIM 83	* IS 125
DIRECT 85	* ISNT 125
DISABLE 145	
DURATION 25	* LEAVE 54
DURING 39	LENGTH 153
ELSE 68	MAX 84
ENABLE 145	MIN 11
END 28, 126	MODEND 18
	MODULE 18

2. USE OF DATA TYPES

The following table shows for every data type whether an object of this type may be used

- as element of an array

- as component of a structure

- as parameter of a procedure

- as result of a procedure

- as value of a reference variable

- as transfer item of data stations

- together with the invariant attribute

- global

- together with the initial attribute.

Type	array element	structure component	parameter	result	value of references	transfer item	INV	GLOBAL	INIT
FIXED	x	x	x	x	x	x	x	x	x
FLOAT	x	x	x	x	x	x	x	x	x
BIT	x	x	x	x	x	x	x	x	x
CHAR	x	x	x	x	x	x	x	x	x
CLOCK	x	x	x	x	x	x	x	x	x
DUR	x	x	x	x	x	x	x	x	x
SEMA	x	-	x	-	x	-	-	x	-
BOLT	x	-	x	-	x	-	-	x	-
IRPT	x	-	x	-	x	-	-	x	-
SIGNAL	x	-	x	-	x	-	-	x	-
DATION	x	-	x	-	x	-	-	x	-
array	-	x	x	-	x	-	x	x	x
structure	x	x	x	x	x	x	x	x	x
new type	x	x	x	x	x	x	x	x	x
REF	x	x	x	x	-	-	-	x	-
PROC	-	-	-	-	-	-	-	x	-
TASK	-	-	-	-	-	-	-	x	-
FORMAT	-	-	-	-	-	-	-	-	-

Objects of type **SEMA** , **BOLT** , **IRPT** , **SIGNAL** , **DATION** , array, **STRUCT** or of new type must be specified with **IDENT** if they are to be used as formal parameters of procedures.

3. SYNTAX LIST

In order to specify the extensions of the described subset of Full PEARL with respect to Basic PEARL the relevant rules are marked with one or two asterisks having the following meaning:

*   This rule produces a phrase, which is restricted in Basic PEARL.

      E.g.   *   260   problem-division   ::=

                    PROBLEM;   (/ declaration / specification /)$^{...}$

           In Basic PEARL a special sequence has to be kept for declarations and specifications.

**   This rule produces a phrase, which is not allowed at all in Basic PEARL.

      E.g.   **   660   type-declaration   ::=

                    TYPE identifier structure-mode;

3.1   Basic Elements, Program

10   digit ::=
          0/1/2/3/4/5/6/7/8/9

20   letter ::=
          A/B/C/D/E/F/G/H/I/J/K/L/M/N/O/P/Q/R/S/T/U/V/W/X/Y/Z

30   identifier ::=
          letter (/ letter / digit /)$^{...}$

40   constant-denotation ::=
          integer-constant-denotation /
          real-constant-denotation /
          bit-string-constant-denotation /
          character-string-constant-denotation /
          clock-constant-denotation /
          duration-constant-denotation

50   integer-constant-denotation ::=
         simple-integer-constant-denotation (/ (precision) /)

60   simple-integer-constant-denotation ::=
         digit⋯ / (0/1)⋯B

70   precision ::=
         simple-integer-constant-denotation

80   real-constant-denotation ::=
         simple-real-constant-denotation (/ (precision) /)

90   simple-real-constant-denotation ::=
         $\left\{ \begin{array}{l} \left\{ \begin{array}{l} (/\ \text{digit}^{⋯}\ /).\text{digit}^{⋯} \\ \text{digit}^{⋯}. \end{array} \right\}\ (/\ \text{exponent-part}\ /) \\ \text{digit}^{⋯}\ \text{exponent-part} \end{array} \right\}$

100   exponent-part ::=
         E ((/ + /) / -) (/ digit /) digit

* 110 bit-string-constant-denotation ::=
         $\left\{ \begin{array}{l} \text{'B1-digit}^{⋯⋯}\text{' (B/B1)} \\ \text{'B2-digit}^{⋯⋯}\text{' B2} \\ \text{'B3-digit}^{⋯⋯}\text{' B3} \\ \text{'B4-digit}^{⋯⋯}\text{' B4} \end{array} \right\}$

120   B1-digit ::=
         0/1

** 130 B2-digit ::=
         0/1/2/3

140   B3-digit ::=
         0/1/2/3/4/5/6/7

150   B4-digit ::=
         0/1/2/3/4/5/6/7/8/9/A/B/C/D/E/F

160   character-string-denotation ::=
         ' (character-without-apostrophe /'')⋯ '

170   character-without-apostrophe ::=

        digit/letter/␣/+/-/*/ / / (/) / [/] /:/./;/,/=/</ >

180   clock-constant-denotation ::=

        simple-integer-constant-denotation§for-hours :

        simple-integer-constant-denotation§for-minutes :

$$\left\{ \begin{array}{l} \text{simple-integer-constant-denotation§for-seconds} \\ \text{simple-real-constant-denotation§for-seconds} \end{array} \right\}$$

190   duration-constant-denotation ::=

$$\left\{ \begin{array}{l} \text{hours}\ (/\ \text{minutes}\ /)\ (/\ \text{seconds}\ /) \\ \text{minutes}\ (/\ \text{seconds}\ /) \\ \text{seconds} \end{array} \right\}$$

200   hours ::=

        simple-integer-constant-denotation **HRS**

210   minutes ::=

        simple-integer-constant-denotation **MIN**

220   seconds ::=

$$\left\{ \begin{array}{l} \text{simple-integer-constant-denotation} \\ \text{simple-real-constant-denotation} \end{array} \right\} \textbf{SEC}$$

230   program ::=

        module"""

* 240   module ::=

        MODULE (/ (identifier) /);

$$\left\{ \begin{array}{l} \text{system-division}\ (/\ \text{problem-division}\ /) \\ \text{problem-division} \end{array} \right\}$$

        MODEND;

3.2   Problem Division

* 250   problem-division ::=

        PROBLEM; (/ declaration / specification /)```

3.2.1 Declarations

* 260   declaration ::=

        length-definition /

        declare-sentence /

        procedure-declaration /

        task-declaration /

        remote-format-declaration /

        type-definition /

        operator-declaration /

        precedence-definition

  270   length-definition ::=

        LENGTH

        (FIXED/FLOAT/BIT/CHAR/CHARACTER) (precision) ;

* 280   declare-sentence ::=

        (DECLARE / DCL)

        (one-identifier-or-list (/ bound-list /)

          (problem-data-attribute / reference-attribute /

           sema-attribute / bolt-attribute / dation-attribute)

        ),``;

  290   one-identifier-or-list ::=

        identifier / (identifier,``)

* 300   bound-list ::=

        (((/ (/ - /) simple-integer-constant-denotation§lower-bound : /)

            (/ - /) simple-integer-constant-denotation§upper-bound

        ),``)

  310   problem-data-attribute ::=

        (/ **INV** /) (simple-mode / structure-mode)

        (/ resident-attribute /) (/ global-attribute /) (/ initial-attribute /)

320   simple-mode ::=

$$\left\{ \begin{array}{l} \left\{ \begin{array}{l} \text{FIXED} \\ \text{FLOAT} \end{array} \right\} \quad (/ \; \underline{(} \text{precision} \underline{)} \; /) \\[2em] \left. \begin{array}{l} \text{BIT} \\ \text{CHAR/CHARACTER} \end{array} \right\} \quad (/ \; \underline{(} \text{length} \underline{)} \; /) \\[1em] \text{DUR/DURATION} \\ \text{CLOCK} \end{array} \right\}$$

330   length ::=
        simple-integer-constant-denotation

* 340   structure-mode ::=
        identifier§user-defined-mode /
        STRUCT [((/ one-identifier-or-list /) mode-in-structure-mode),⋯]

* 350   mode-in-structure-mode ::=
        (/ bound-list /)
        (simple-mode / structure-mode / reference-mode)

360   resident-attribute ::=
        RESIDENT

* 370   global-attribute ::=
        GLOBAL (/ $\underline{(}$ identifier§module $\underline{)}$ /)

* 380   initial-attribute ::=
        (**INITIAL** / **INIT**) $\underline{(}$ ((/ +/- /) constant-denotation),⋯ $\underline{)}$

** 390   reference-attribute ::=
        reference-mode (/ resident-attribute /) (/ global-attribute /)

** 400   reference-mode ::=
        REF (/ virt-bound-list /)
        (((/ **INV** /) (simple-mode / structure-mode)) /
        dation-mode / **SEMA** / **BOLT** / **INTERRUPT** / **IRPT** / **SIGNAL**)

164

```
 * 410    virt-bound-list  ::=
                  ( (/ , ··· /) )

   420    sema-attribute  ::=
                  SEMA (/ resident-attribute /) (/ global-attribute /)
                  (/ PRESET ( simple-integer-constant-denotation, ·· ) /)

** 430    bolt-attribute  ::=
                  BOLT (/ resident-attribute /) (/ global-attribute /)

   440    dation-attribute  ::=
                  dation-mode (/ resident-attribute /) (/ global-attribute /)
                  CREATED ( name§system-defined-dation )

   450    dation-mode  ::=
                  DATION sink-source-attribute class
                  (/ topology access /) (/ control-attribute /)

   460    sink-source-attribute  ::=
                  IN / OUT / INOUT

   470    class  ::=
                  ALPHIC / BASIC / transfer-item-type

 * 480    transfer-item-type  ::=
                  ALL / simple-mode / compound-mode

 * 490    compound-mode  ::=
                  structure-mode-for-IO / identifier§user-defined-mode

   500    structure-mode-for-IO  ::=
                  STRUCT [structure-component-for-IO , ·· ]

 * 510    structure-component-for-IO  ::=
                  (/ one-identifier-or-list /)
                  (simple-mode / structure-mode-for-IO /
                  identifier§user-defined-mode-for-IO)
```

520 topology ::=

  DIM ((/ * / integer-constant-denotation /)

    (/ , (/ integer-constant-denotation /)

    (/ , (/ integer-constant-denotation /) /) /))

  (/ TFU (/ MAX /) /)

530 access ::=

  (DIRECT / FORWARD / FORBACK)

  ((/ NOCYCL /) / CYCLIC)

  ((/ STREAM /) / NOSTREAM)

540 control-attribute ::=

  CONTROL (ALL)

550 procedure-declaration ::=

  identifier : (PROCEDURE / PROC)

    (/ list-of-formal-parameters /)

    (/ result-attribute /)

    (/ resident-attribute /)

    (/ reentrant-attribute /)

    (/ global-attribute /) ;

    procedure-body

    END;

* 560 list-of-formal-parameters ::=

  ((one-identifier-or-list (/ virt-bound-list /)

   parameter-mode (/ IDENT / IDENTICAL /)),")

* 570 parameter-mode ::=

  ((/ INV /) (simple-mode / structure-mode)) /

  reference-mode / SEMA / BOLT / INTERRUPT / IRPT /

  SIGNAL / dation-mode

* 580 result-attribute ::=

  RETURNS (simple-mode / structure-mode / reference- mode)

590 reentrant-attribute ::=

  REENT

* 600 procedure-body ::=

  (/ declaration··· /) (/ statement··· /)

```
610   task-declaration  ::=
          identifier : TASK (/ priority /)
          (/ resident-attribute /) (/ global-attribute /) ;
          procedure-body
          END;

620   priority  ::=
          (PRIORITY / PRIO) integer-constant-denotation

630   remote-format-declaration  ::=
          identifier : FORMAT ( format-or-position ,** ) ;

** 640   type-definition ::=
          TYPE identifier structure-mode;

** 650   operator-declaration  ::=
          OPERATOR op-name ( (/ op-parameter , /) op-parameter )
          result-attribute;
          procedure-body
          END;

** 660   op-name  ::=
          identifier / + / - / * / / / ** / // / = / == / / = /<= />= /</>/<>/><

** 670   op-parameter  ::=
          identifier (/ virt-bound-list /) parameter-mode (/ IDENT / IDENTICAL /)

** 680   precedence-definition ::=
          PRECEDENCE op-name ( 1/2/3/4/5/6/7 );
```

167

3.2.2 Specifications

```
690    specification  ::=
                (SPECIFY / SPC)
                (one-identifier-or-list
                 (spc-attribute /
                  proc-spc-attribute /
                  task-spc-attribute)
                ),";

* 700  spc-attribute  ::=
                (/ virt-bound-list /)
                ( ( (/ INV /) (simple-mode / structure-mode) ) /
                    reference-mode / SEMA / BOLT / INTERRUPT / IRPT /
                    SIGNAL / dation-mode)
                (/ resident-attribute /) (/ global-attribute /)

  710  proc-spc-attribute  ::=
                procedure-mode
                (/ resident-attribute /) (/ reentrant-attribute /) global-attribute

* 720  procedure-mode  ::=
                ENTRY
                (/ ( ( (/ virt-bound-list /) parameter-mode (/ IDENTICAL / IDENT /) ),") /)
                (/ result-attribute /)

* 730  task-spc-attribute  ::=
                TASK  (/ resident-attribute /) global-attribute
```

3.2.3 Statements

```
740    statement  ::=
                (/ identifier§label : /)··· unlabelled-statement

750    unlabelled-statement  ::=
                assignment / block / sequential-control-statement /
                realtime-statement / IO-statement
```

```
* 760    assignment  ::=
                ⎧ name            ⎫
                ⎨ dereferencing   ⎬  ( := / = ) ··  expression ;
                ⎩ string-selection ⎭

* 770    name  ::=
                (identifier (/ ( index ,·· ) /) ).··

  780    index  ::=
                expression§which-yields-an-integer

* 790    string-selection  ::=
                name§string . (BIT / CHAR / CHARACTER )
                ( (integer-constant-denotation (/ : integer-constant-denotation /) ) ) /
                 (identifier (/ : identifier + integer-constant-denotation /) ) )

** 800   dereferencing  ::=
                CONT (name§reference / function-call)

  810    expression  ::=
                (/ monadic-operator /) operand dyadic-operator··

* 820    monadic-operator  ::=
                + / - / identifier§monadic-operator

* 830    dyadic-operator  ::=
                + / - / * / / / // / /// / ** / < / > / < = / > = / == / /= / >< / < >/
                identifier§dyadic-operator

* 840    operand  ::=
                constant-denotation / name / function-call / conditional-expression /
                dereferencing / string-selection / ( expression ) / ( assignment )

  850    function-call  ::=
                identifier§function (/ list-of-actual-parameters /)

  860    list-of-actual-parameters  ::=
                ( expression ,·· )

** 870   conditional-expression  ::=
                IF expression THEN expression ELSE expression FIN
```

169

* 880   block ::=
          BEGIN (/ declaration··· /) (/ statement··· /) END;

  890   sequential-control-statement ::=
          goto-statement / if-statement / case-statement /
          dummy-statement / loop-statement / call-statement / return-statement

* 900   goto-statement ::=
          GOTO identifier§label ;

  910   if-statement ::=
          IF expression§which-yields-bit1
          THEN statement··· (/ ELSE statement··· /) FIN;

  920   case-statement ::=
          CASE expression§which-yields-an-integer
          (ALT statement···)···
          (/ OUT statement··· /)
          FIN;

  930   dummy-statement ::=
          ;

* 940   loop-statement ::=
          (/ FOR identifier§loop-variable /)
          (/ FROM expression§start /)
          (/ BY expression§step /)
          (/ TO expression§end /)
          (/ WHILE expression§condition /)
          REPEAT
          (/ declaration··· /) (/ statement··· /)
          END;

  950   call-statement ::=
          CALL identifier§procedure (/ list-of-actual-parameters /);

  960   return-statement ::=
          RETURN (/ (expression) /);

970   realtime-statement ::=

       task-statement / synchronizer-operation / interrupt-operation /
       signal-operation

980   task-statement ::=

       activate-statement / terminate-statement / suspend-statement /
       continue-statement / resume-statement / prevent-statement

* 990   activate-statement ::=

       (/ schedule /) **ACTIVATE** identifier§task (/ priority /);

*1000   schedule ::=

$$\left\{ \begin{array}{l} \textbf{AT } \text{expression§time (/ frequence /)} \\ \textbf{AFTER } \text{expression§duration (/ frequence /)} \\ \textbf{WHEN } \text{name§interrupt (/ } \textbf{AFTER } \text{expression§duration /) (/ frequence /)} \\ \text{frequence} \end{array} \right\}$$

1010   frequence ::=

       ALL expression§duration
       (/ (**UNTIL** expression§time) / (**DURING** expression§duration) /)

1020   terminate-statement ::=

       TERMINATE (/ identifier§task /);

*1030   suspend-statement ::=

       SUSPEND (/ identifier§task /);

*1040   continue-statement ::=

       (/ **AT** expression§time /
        AFTER expression§duration /
        WHEN name§interrupt /)
       CONTINUE ((identifier§task (/ priority /)) / priority);

1050   resume-statement ::=

       (**AT** expression§time /
        AFTER expression§duration /
       WHEN name§interrupt)
       RESUME;

```
1060  prevent-statement  ::=
          PREVENT (/ identifier§task /);

*1070  synchronizer-operation  ::=
          ⎧  REQUEST  name§sema ,¨;  ⎫
          ⎪  RELEASE  name§sema , ¨;  ⎪
          ⎨  RESERVE  name§bolt ,¨;   ⎬
          ⎪  FREE  name§bolt ,¨;      ⎪
          ⎪  ENTER  name§bolt ,¨;     ⎪
          ⎩  LEAVE  name§bolt ,¨;     ⎭

*1080  interrupt-operation  ::=
          ⎧  ENABLE  name§interrupt ;  ⎫
          ⎨  DISABLE name§interrupt ;  ⎬
          ⎩  TRIGGER name§interrupt ;  ⎭

1090  signal-operation  ::=
          ⎧  ON  name§signal ,¨ : unlabelled-statement  ⎫
          ⎨  INDUCE  name§signal ;                      ⎬
          ⎩                                             ⎭

1100  IO-statement  ::=
          open-statement / close-statement /
          read-statement / write-statement /
          get-statement / put-statement /
          take-statement / send-statement

1110  open-statement  ::=
          OPEN  name§dation (/ BY open-parameter ,¨ /) ;

* 1120  open-parameter  ::=
          (IDF ( (name§character-string / character-string-constant-denotation) ) ) /
          OLD / NEW / ANY / CAN / PRM

1130  close-statement  ::=
          CLOSE  name§dation (/ BY close-parameter ,¨ /) ;

**1140  close-parameter  ::=
          CAN / PRM
```

1150 read-statement ::=
      READ (/ (name / slice) ,`"` /) **FROM** name§dation
      (/ **BY** position ,`"` /);

1160 slice ::=
      identifier§array
      ((/ - /) simple-integer-constant-denotation :
       (/ - /) simple-integer-constant-denotation)

1170 position ::=
$$\left\{ \begin{array}{l} \text{(COL / LINE) (expression)} \\ \text{POS (expression (/ , expression (/ , expression /) /))} \\ \text{(X / SKIP / PAGE) (/ (expression) /)} \\ \text{ADV (expression (/ , expression (/ , expression /) /))} \end{array} \right\}$$

1180 write-statement ::=
      WRITE (/ (expression / slice) ,`"` /) **TO** name§dation
      (/ **BY** position ,`"` /);

1190 get-statement ::=
      GET (/ (name / slice) ,`"` /) **FROM** name§dation
      (/ **BY** format-or-position ,`"` /) ;

1200 format-or-position ::=
$$\left\{ \begin{array}{l} \text{(/ mult /) (format / position)} \\ \text{mult (format-or-position ,}`"`\text{)} \end{array} \right\}$$

*1210 mult ::=
      (expression§which-yields-an-integer)

*1220 format ::=
$$\left\{ \begin{array}{l} \text{(F / E) (expression (/ , expression (/ , expression /) /))} \\ \text{(B / B1 / B2 / B3 / B4 / A) (/ (expression) /)} \\ \text{(T / D) (expression (/ , expression /))} \\ \text{LIST} \\ \text{R (identifier§format)} \end{array} \right\}$$

1230 put-statement ::=
      PUT (/ (expression / slice) ,`"` /) **TO** name§dation
      (/ **BY** format-or-position ,`"` /) ;

173

1240 take-statement ::=

 TAKE (/ (name / slice) ,·· /) FROM name§dation
 (/ BY format-or-position ,·· /) ;

1250 send-statement ::=

 SEND (/ (expression / slice) ,·· /) TO name§dation
 (/ BY format-or-position ,·· /) ;

3.3   System Division

1260 system-division ::=

 SYSTEM ; (/ connection ··· /)

1270 connection ::=

$$
\text{connection-point} \ (/ \left\{ \begin{array}{l} \left\{ \begin{array}{l} \text{->} \\ \text{< -} \\ \text{<->} \end{array} \right\} \ (/ \ \text{connection-point} \ +^{··} \ /) \\ + \ \text{connection-point} \ +^{··} \end{array} \right\} \ /) ;
$$

*1280 connection-point ::=

 (/ user-name : /)··· (/ system-name /)

$$
(/ * \left\{ \begin{array}{l} \text{identifier§point} \\ \text{int§point} \\ \underline{(}\ \text{int : int} \ (/ \underline{/}\ \text{int§step} \ /) \ \underline{)} \end{array} \right\} \ (/ \ , \ \text{int§width} \ /) \ /)
$$

1290 int ::=

 integer-constant-denotation

1300 user-name ::=

 identifier (/ (int : int) /)

1310 system-name ::=

 identifier (/ (int (/ : int /)) /)

174

4. EXTENSIONS WITH RESPECT TO BASIC PEARL

This paragraph lists functionally the essential extensions of the PEARL subset of Werum with respect to Basic PEARL (Standard 78).

Data Types

- REF
- user defined types (TYPE)
- BOLT
- arrays with elements of type SEMA , BOLT , REF , user defined DATION , STRUCT , user defined type (TYPE)
- arrays with more than 3 dimensions
- arrays with lower bounds < 1
- structures with components of type array , STRUCT , REF , user defined type (TYPE)
- B2 bit strings

Declarations, Specifications, Definitions

- Modules may be identified (e.g. MODULE (TEST))
- Global attribute with module identifier (e.g. ...GLOBAL (TEST))
- Definition of new data types (TYPE)
- Declaration of new operators (OPERATOR) with precedences (PRECEDENCE)
- Declarations and specifications may be made in arbitrary sequence
- Local procedures, i.e. declaration of procedures also within tasks, procedures, blocks and loops
- Objects of type SEMA , BOLT , IRPT , SIGNAL , REF and user defined type (TYPE) may be parameters of procedures

- Objects of type **REF** , **STRUCT** and user defined type (**TYPE**) may be results of function procedures

- Long forms of **INIT** and **IDENT** : **INITIAL** , **IDENTICAL**.

- Objects of type array, **STRUCT** and user defined type (**TYPE**) may be initialised in their declaration with the **INITIAL** attribute.

Statements

- Values of reference variables and character string slices at the left side of assignments
  (e.g. STRING.**CHAR** (J) := 'N' ;)

- The schedule of an activate statement may be combined with a frequence and/or **AFTER** duration
  (e.g. **WHEN** interrupt **AFTER** duration **ALL** duration
        DURING duration **ACTIVATE** task ;)

- **SUSPEND** for other tasks

- **CONTINUE** with priority change

- Lists of **SEMA** variables after **REQUEST** and **RELEASE**

- **BOLT** statements **ENTER** , **LEAVE** , **RESERVE** , **FREE**

- Lists of **BOLT** variables in bolt statements

- **TRIGGER** statement.

Expressions

- Slices of character strings, variable slices of strings
  (e.g. X := INPUT.**BIT** (I : I + 3) ;
        OUTPUT.**CHAR** (J) := STRING.**CHAR** (K) ;)

- Dereferenciation (**CONT**)

- Conditional expression
  (e.g. A := **IF** B > 1 **THEN** B **ELSE** C **FIN** ;)

- Monadic operators LWB and UPB.

Input/Output

- **STRUCT** , user defined type (**TYPE**) and **ALL** may be transfer item type

- Arrays of user defined data stations

- Open parameter CAN , PRM

- Close parameter CAN , PRM

System Division

- Arbitrary sequence of connections

- Inverse notation of connections

- Identifier and / step possible after * in connection points.

5. RESTRICTIONS WITH RESPECT TO FULL PEARL

This paragraph lists shortly the essential restrictions of the PEARL
subset of Werum with respect to Full PEARL (Standard 80).

Data Types

- Only static array bounds

- Slices only within I/O statements and only with static bounds

- Character strings only with static bounds

- No replicators in bit and character string constant denotations

- No data types necessary for user defined interfaces.

Declarations, Specifications, Definitions

- **LENGTH** definition only at module level

- Declaration and specification of data stations only at module level

- **IDENTICAL** attribute only in context with parameters

- Only constants within the **INITIAL** attribute

- No **INLINE** procedures.

Statements

- Only positive integers as task priorities

- No lists of schedules

- **SUSPEND**, **TERMINATE**, **PREVENT** only without schedule

- **CONTINUE** only with simple schedules

- **RESUME** only for the executing task.

Expressions

- No interrupt slices

- No array displays and structure displays.

Input/Output

-   No user defined interfaces between data stations (with all impli-
    cations)

-   No arrays and **ONEOF** as transfer item type.

Keywords

The following keywords of Full PEARL are not part of the PEARL
subset of Werum:

CREATE	MATCH
DELETE	NOMATCH
EVERY	ONEOF
EXIT	UPON
INLINE	USING
INTFAC	

INDEX

180

Günther Lamprecht

Introduction to SIMULA 67

1981. IV, 234 p. DIN C 5. Pb.

SIMULA is a high level language developed during the years 1965 −1967 and basing on the programming language ALGOL 60. Although the name SIMULA mainly points to the programming of simulation models the language can be used to program other data processing problems as well.

The handling of texts in SIMULA is much easier than it is with ALGOL 60. The new concept of classes not only allows the description of structures ("objects"), but also to understand classes as generalized procedures which may be processed simultaneously as coroutines and which can call each other. Finally it is possible to build-up and organize sets ("lists") in a very easy way.

The present "Introduction to SIMULA" explains the facilities of that programming language starting from the problems to be solved. The reader will proceed from simple problems to complex ones, finding solutions and additional explanations to all exercises and examples. Thus, he will learn the programming languages SIMULA very easily.

The manufacturer's authorised representative in the EU is Springer
Nature Customer Service Centre GmbH, Europaplatz 3, 69115 Heidelberg,
Germany. If you have any concerns regarding our products, please
contact ProductSafety@springernature.com

Printed and bound by CPI Group (UK) Ltd, Croydon, CR0 4YY
28/04/2026
02098512-0004